I0018811

i

To everyone who's ever struggled with organizing their digital life — may OneDrive make your creative journey a little easier and a lot more inspired.

Table of Contents

Introduction

Welcome to the Digital Art Revolution

The way artists create, store, and share their work has changed dramatically in recent years. Gone are the days when an artist's portfolio consisted of physical prints stored in a binder or carefully packed canvases waiting for an exhibition. Today, digital technology allows artists to showcase their work online, reaching global audiences with just a few clicks.

As an artist, your creative work is valuable. Whether you are a painter, illustrator, photographer, graphic designer, or digital artist, having an organized, secure, and easily accessible digital portfolio is essential. Cloud storage services like OneDrive offer a powerful way to store, manage, and present your artwork professionally while ensuring that your files are protected and always available when needed.

This book will guide you through the process of using OneDrive to build and maintain a digital art portfolio that is efficient, visually appealing, and easy to share. Whether you are a beginner in cloud storage or someone looking to optimize your existing workflow, you will find step-by-step instructions, expert insights, and practical tips to help you make the most of OneDrive for your artistic career.

Why OneDrive? – Benefits of Using OneDrive for Artists

When it comes to storing and sharing digital artwork, there are several cloud storage options available. However, OneDrive stands out as an excellent choice for artists due to its unique combination of security, accessibility, and powerful organizational features.

Key Advantages of Using OneDrive for Artists

- **Secure and Reliable Storage**
  Your artwork is not just another set of files—it represents your creativity, effort, and artistic vision. OneDrive ensures that your files are protected against accidental loss, device failures, or theft by securely storing them in the cloud.

- **Seamless Accessibility Across Devices**
  Whether you are working on a digital painting at your studio, reviewing your portfolio on a tablet, or showcasing your work on a phone, OneDrive keeps your files synchronized across all your devices. This means you can access your artwork anytime, anywhere, without worrying about carrying physical storage drives.

- **Easy Organization and Management**
  Organizing your artwork is crucial for efficient workflow. OneDrive allows you to create structured folders, add metadata, and use advanced search features to quickly find specific pieces, making it an ideal tool for keeping track of your work.

- **Professional Portfolio Sharing**
  Artists need to share their work with clients, collectors, and potential buyers. OneDrive provides simple yet powerful sharing options that let you control who can view, download, or comment on your portfolio, ensuring a professional presentation of your work.

- **Version Control for Artwork Edits**
  Creative projects often go through multiple revisions. With OneDrive's version history feature, you can track changes in your artwork, restore previous versions, and avoid losing important modifications.
- **Collaboration with Clients and Other Artists**
  If you work with art buyers, design teams, or fellow creatives, OneDrive enables real-time collaboration, allowing multiple people to review, edit, and comment on files without endless email exchanges.

By the end of this book, you will understand how to harness these features to store, manage, and showcase your digital art portfolio with confidence.

Who Is This Book For?

This book is designed for artists of all backgrounds and skill levels who want to take control of their digital artwork and build an organized, professional portfolio using OneDrive. It is especially useful for:

- Digital Artists and Illustrators who need a structured way to store and present their work online.
- Traditional Artists who want to digitize and archive their paintings, drawings, and sculptures.
- Photographers looking for a secure cloud-based system to manage and share their photo collections.
- Graphic Designers and Creators who work with clients and need a reliable collaboration tool.

- Art Students and Hobbyists seeking to develop an online portfolio for future opportunities.
- Freelancers and Professionals who need an efficient way to manage, showcase, and sell their artwork.

If you belong to any of these categories—or if you simply want to understand how to manage your creative assets more efficiently—this book is for you.

How to Use This Book

This book is structured as a step-by-step guide, ensuring that every topic is explained clearly before moving on to more advanced concepts. Whether you are new to OneDrive or already have some experience with cloud storage, you will find valuable insights and techniques to improve the way you organize and share your artwork.

Here's how you can get the most out of this book:

- **Follow the Chapters in Order**
  Each section builds on the previous one. It is recommended that you read the chapters in sequence to gain a full understanding of how to use OneDrive effectively.
- **Apply What You Learn**
  The best way to master OneDrive is through practice. As you progress through the book, try implementing the techniques on your own artwork.
- **Use This as a Reference Guide**
  Even after completing the book, you can return to specific chapters for quick guidance on particular topics, such as sharing portfolios or recovering lost files.
- **Take Notes and Experiment**
  Everyone has a different creative workflow. Feel free to adapt the strategies in this book to fit your unique artistic process.

By following these principles, you will not only learn how to use OneDrive but also create a well-structured and highly effective digital art portfolio that enhances your professional presence.

What You Will Learn

By the end of this book, you will have a deep understanding of how to:

- **Set Up and Navigate OneDrive Efficiently**
  Learn how to create an account, organize files, and use OneDrive's key features to store and access your artwork effortlessly.
- **Create and Manage a Digital Art Portfolio**
  Discover how to structure your portfolio in a way that showcases your work professionally, attracts clients, and makes navigation easy.
- **Optimize and Edit Art Files**
  Explore built-in tools and external software integrations that allow you to enhance, resize, and adjust your artwork before sharing it.
- **Share Your Work with Clients and Art Collectors**
  Master the best ways to distribute, present, and protect your portfolio while maintaining control over access permissions.
- **Secure and Back Up Your Digital Creations**
  Understand how to protect your artwork from loss, theft, and accidental deletions by using OneDrive's security and recovery options.
- **Sell and License Your Artwork Online**
  Get insights into how to use OneDrive for digital file deliveries, licensing agreements, and online art sales.

This book will equip you with the knowledge and skills needed to take full advantage of OneDrive as a digital art management tool—allowing you to store, organize, showcase, and share your creations with confidence.

Part 1: Getting Started with OneDrive

Chapter 1: Introduction to OneDrive for Artists

Digital art, photography, paintings, graphic design, and other creative works have evolved alongside technology, making it essential for artists to have a reliable and organized system for storing, managing, and sharing their work. OneDrive, Microsoft's cloud storage service, provides an efficient and user-friendly way for artists to securely store their portfolios, access them from anywhere, and collaborate seamlessly.

This chapter introduces OneDrive, explores its benefits for artists, compares free and paid plans, and provides step-by-step guidance on setting up an account.

What Is OneDrive?

OneDrive is a **cloud-based storage service** that allows users to save, manage, and share files online. Instead of storing all your artwork and projects on a single computer or external hard drive, OneDrive enables you to **access your files from any device**, as long as you have an internet connection.

With OneDrive, your work is not only **stored safely in the cloud** but is also protected against accidental loss due to hardware failures or unexpected issues like stolen devices or corrupted files. It functions as a **virtual storage drive**, ensuring that your creative work is always accessible when you need it.

Key Features of OneDrive for Artists

- **Cloud-Based Storage** – Store your digital artwork, photos, and designs securely online without taking up space on your computer.
- **Seamless Accessibility** – Access your artwork from a desktop, laptop, tablet, or smartphone.
- **Automatic Syncing** – Ensure all your files are always up to date across all your devices.
- **File Versioning** – Retrieve previous versions of your work, allowing you to undo changes or compare different versions.
- **Collaboration Tools** – Easily share files with clients, galleries, and collaborators without worrying about email attachment limits.
- **Robust Security** – Keep your work safe with Microsoft's advanced encryption and security features.

By using OneDrive, artists can **streamline their workflow**, protect their creative assets, and share their portfolios effortlessly.

Why Artists Should Use Cloud Storage

Traditionally, artists have stored their work on personal computers, external hard drives, or USB devices. While these methods provide direct access to files, they come with **several limitations and risks**, including **device failures, file corruption, and loss of work** due to theft or accidents.

Cloud storage, especially OneDrive, eliminates these risks and offers a **convenient and efficient way to manage artwork**. Here's why artists should consider using OneDrive:

1. Protection Against Data Loss

Hard drives can fail, USB drives can be lost, and computers can crash. OneDrive provides **a secure, cloud-based backup** that ensures your files are always safe, even if something happens to your physical devices.

2. Access Artwork from Anywhere

Whether you are working on a new piece at home, showcasing your portfolio at an exhibition, or traveling for inspiration, OneDrive **lets you access your files from any device**.

3. Easy File Sharing and Collaboration

Sharing large image files through email can be difficult due to size restrictions. With OneDrive, artists can **generate shareable links** to send to clients, buyers, or collaborators without worrying about file size limitations.

4. Secure and Private Storage

Unlike social media platforms where artwork can be copied or used without permission, OneDrive provides **secure, private storage** where only you and those you grant access to can view or download your work.

5. Organized and Efficient Portfolio Management

OneDrive allows you to **create folders, albums, and tags** to keep your artwork neatly categorized, making it easier to find and showcase specific pieces.

6. Automatic Synchronization and Version Control

Artists frequently make revisions to their work. OneDrive keeps track of **file versions**, allowing you to restore previous iterations of an artwork if needed.

These advantages make OneDrive a **powerful tool for artists**, enabling them to **preserve, access, and share their work effortlessly**.

Free vs. Paid OneDrive Plans – Choosing the Right Plan

OneDrive offers **both free and paid plans**, and choosing the right one depends on your storage needs and workflow requirements.

Free OneDrive Plan (Basic)

Microsoft provides **5GB of free cloud storage** with a basic OneDrive account. This is a good option for artists who:

- Need a place to store a small number of digital artworks or photography collections.
- Are just starting with cloud storage and want to test its functionality.

- Have external storage options and only require limited cloud storage.

However, 5GB can fill up quickly, especially for artists working with **high-resolution images, PSD files, or video-based artwork.**

Paid OneDrive Plans (Subscription-Based)

For artists who need **more storage and advanced features**, Microsoft offers paid plans that provide:

- **More storage space** – Up to **1TB (1,000GB) or more**, depending on the plan.
- **Additional features** – Such as advanced security, automatic backups, and integration with Microsoft Office apps.

Key Paid Plan Options:

- **OneDrive Standalone 100GB Plan** – Provides 100GB of storage but does not include Microsoft Office.
- **Microsoft 365 Personal Plan** – Includes 1TB of storage plus access to Office apps like Word, Excel, and PowerPoint.
- **Microsoft 365 Family Plan** – Offers 1TB per user (up to 6 users), making it ideal for artists who work in teams.

Which Plan Should You Choose?

- If you are **a beginner or casual artist**, the **free 5GB plan** might be sufficient for storing and organizing a limited number of artworks.

- If you create **high-resolution digital paintings, photography, or 3D models**, a **100GB or 1TB plan** is a better choice.
- If you collaborate frequently, use Office tools, or need **large amounts of cloud storage**, the **Microsoft 365 Personal or Family plan** is ideal.

Selecting the right plan ensures you have **enough space to store, manage, and share your creative work** without limitations.

Setting Up Your OneDrive Account

Before you can start using OneDrive to store and organize your artwork, you need to create an account. The setup process is straightforward and requires only a few steps.

Step 1: Visit the OneDrive Website or Download the App

- Go to **onedrive.com** on your web browser.
- Alternatively, **download the OneDrive app** from the Microsoft Store (Windows), App Store (iOS), or Google Play (Android).

☁ Microsoft OneDrive   ×

Set up OneDrive

Put your files in OneDrive to get them from any device.

enter your email address

| enter your email address |

| Create account | Sign in

Step 2: Sign In or Create a Microsoft Account

- If you already have a Microsoft account (Outlook, Hotmail, or Xbox account), use it to **sign in** to OneDrive.
- If you don't have an account, click on **"Sign Up"** and follow the prompts to create one.

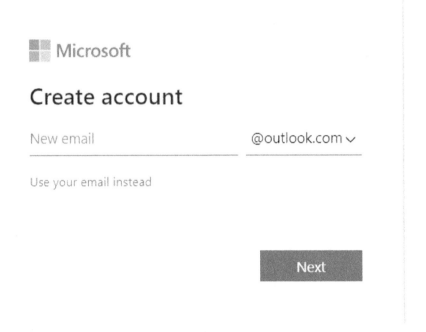

Step 3: Choose Your OneDrive Plan

- Select **either the free plan or a paid subscription** based on your needs.
- If opting for a paid plan, enter your payment details and confirm your subscription.

Step 4: Set Up OneDrive on Your Computer

- If using **Windows**, OneDrive is **built-in** and can be accessed from **File Explorer**.
- If using **Mac**, download and install the OneDrive app from the **Mac App Store**.

Step 5: Start Uploading Your Artwork

- Click the **"Upload" button** to begin adding your artwork, illustrations, or photos to OneDrive.
- Organize your files into folders to **keep your portfolio structured and easy to navigate**.

Step 6: Sync Your Files Across Devices

- Enable **automatic syncing** so that any updates you make to your artwork on one device reflect on all connected devices.

Conclusion

OneDrive is a **powerful and essential tool** for artists looking to store, manage, and share their creative work efficiently. By **understanding its features, choosing the right plan, and setting up an account**, you can ensure that your artwork remains **secure, accessible, and well-organized**.

Chapter 2: Navigating the OneDrive Interface

OneDrive is designed to provide a simple yet powerful way to store, organize, and manage files in the cloud. Before diving into advanced features like sharing, collaboration, and portfolio creation, it is essential to understand the interface and how everything is structured.

In this chapter, we will go through the layout of OneDrive, the different types of files and folders it supports, and how to sync your files across multiple devices. By the end, you should feel comfortable navigating OneDrive's interface and using it effectively to manage your digital artwork.

Overview of the OneDrive Dashboard

When you log into OneDrive through a web browser or open the OneDrive desktop application, you are greeted with the main dashboard. This is the central hub where you can access all your stored files, upload new ones, and organize them into folders.

The OneDrive dashboard consists of the following key sections:

Navigation Pane (Left Sidebar)

- This section provides quick access to important areas like My Files, Recent, Shared, and Recycle Bin.
- It helps you jump between different views and manage your content efficiently.

Main File Display Area (Center Panel)

- This section shows all your uploaded files and folders.
- You can switch between list view (for a structured look) and thumbnail view (for a more visual layout, ideal for artists and designers).

Toolbar (Top Menu Bar)

- The top bar contains options such as Upload, New Folder, Share, Download, and Sort to help you manage your files quickly.
- The search bar allows you to find files instantly by name, keyword, or metadata.

Account & Settings (Top Right Corner)

- This is where you can check storage space, access settings, and sign in or out of your account.
- You can adjust preferences like sync settings, backup preferences, and security options.

Navigating the Dashboard Effectively

- To upload a file, click the "Upload" button and select the files from your device.
- To create a new folder, use the "New" button, then select "Folder" and give it a name.
- Use the search bar to quickly find specific files by name or content.
- Right-click on any file to access quick actions like Rename, Move, Share, or Delete.

By familiarizing yourself with these elements, you will be able to manage your digital portfolio efficiently and find your artwork with ease.

Understanding Folders, Files, and Albums

Organizing your artwork is crucial, especially when dealing with hundreds or thousands of images and designs. OneDrive provides folders, files, and albums to help keep everything structured.

Folders: Keeping Your Files Organized

A folder is a container that holds multiple files. Using folders properly can make your portfolio easy to navigate.

Why Use Folders?

- Helps categorize different types of artwork (e.g., sketches, digital paintings, client work).
- Makes it easier to find specific projects without searching through a long list of files.
- Improves workflow by grouping related files together.

How to Create and Manage Folders

- Click the "New" button in OneDrive and select "Folder".

You can add files to OneDrive in many different ways and then get to them from anywhere.

- Name the folder based on its content, such as "Landscape Paintings" or "Illustrations for Clients".

You can add files to OneDrive in many different ways and then get to them from anywhere.

- Drag and drop files into the appropriate folders to keep everything structured.
- Right-click on a folder to rename, move, or share it.

Files: The Foundation of Your Portfolio

Files are the individual pieces of content stored in OneDrive. These include images, documents, videos, and even project files from design software.

Key Features of File Management in OneDrive

- Preview images and documents without downloading them.
- Rename files for better identification and organization.
- Move or copy files between folders with ease.
- Recover accidentally deleted files from the Recycle Bin.

Albums: A More Visual Way to Organize Your Work

Albums in OneDrive provide a gallery-like experience, allowing you to group images together for a curated portfolio. Unlike folders, albums do not move files but simply create a collection that links related images together.

How to Create an Album

- Select multiple image files and click "Add to Album". Alternatively, navigate to **Photos>Albums>Create a new album**
- Give the album a meaningful name, such as "Watercolor Collection" or "3D Design Showcase".
- Share the album with clients, friends, or collaborators.

Using a combination of folders, files, and albums, you can create an efficient system to store and present your artwork effectively.

File Types Supported by OneDrive (JPEG, PNG, PSD, PDF, etc.)

OneDrive supports a wide range of file formats, making it ideal for artists working in different mediums. Understanding these formats will help you choose the best file type for storage, sharing, and showcasing your work.

Common Image Formats

- JPEG (.jpg, .jpeg) – A compressed image format that reduces file size but may sacrifice some quality. Best for web display.
- PNG (.png) – Supports transparency and high-quality images but results in larger file sizes. Ideal for digital artwork.
- GIF (.gif) – A format used for simple animations or low-resolution graphics.
- TIFF (.tif, .tiff) – A high-quality format commonly used for printing but takes up more storage.

Project and Design Files

- PSD (.psd) – Adobe Photoshop file, retains layers and edits. Ideal for ongoing projects.
- AI (.ai) – Adobe Illustrator format, used for vector graphics.
- SVG (.svg) – Scalable vector format for digital designs and illustrations.

Document Formats for Portfolios

- PDF (.pdf) – Best format for creating a structured digital portfolio. Retains high quality and is easy to share.
- DOCX (.docx) – Microsoft Word document, useful for project descriptions or art proposals.

Choosing the right file format ensures better quality, easier sharing, and professional presentation.

Syncing OneDrive Across Devices

One of the biggest advantages of OneDrive is its ability to sync files across multiple devices. This means you can access your artwork on your computer, tablet, or smartphone without manually transferring files.

How Syncing Works

When you upload or edit a file on one device, the changes automatically reflect across all devices connected to your OneDrive account.

This ensures that you always have access to the latest version of your work, whether you're at home, in a studio, or on the go.

Setting Up OneDrive Sync

Download and Install OneDrive

- If using a Windows PC, OneDrive is usually pre-installed.
- For Mac, download the OneDrive app from the Microsoft website.
- On mobile, install the OneDrive app from the App Store or Google Play.

Sign In and Choose Sync Settings

- Open the OneDrive app and sign in with your Microsoft account.
- Choose which folders you want to sync to your device.

Use Automatic Backup for Important Folders

- Enable automatic backup for key folders like Desktop, Documents, and Pictures.
- This ensures that all changes are immediately uploaded to the cloud.

To do this, you need to go through OneDrive settings>sync and backup>manage backup.

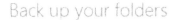

Back up your folders

Selected folders will sync in OneDrive. New and existing files will be added to OneDrive, backed up, and available on your other devices even if you lose this PC. Learn more.

Desktop	Pictures	Documents
162 MB	1 KB	0 KB

Space left in OneDrive after selection: 4.8 GB

Start backup

By syncing your portfolio across devices, you can edit, organize, and showcase your artwork from anywhere without worrying about losing files.

Chapter 3: Uploading and Managing Your Art Portfolio

Managing your art portfolio in a digital space like OneDrive requires understanding the essential steps to ensure that your artwork is stored properly, remains organized, and is easily accessible. This chapter will guide you through the process of uploading, organizing, and tracking changes to your art portfolio, allowing you to manage your creative work efficiently.

How to Upload Files to OneDrive

Uploading files to OneDrive is the first step in making your artwork accessible in the cloud. This process is straightforward, but it's essential to understand the different methods available for uploading, as well as the nuances of managing large art files.

Why Upload to OneDrive? OneDrive allows you to store your files securely while offering seamless access across multiple devices. This ensures that your portfolio can be viewed and updated from anywhere. Uploading your art to OneDrive eliminates the risk of losing files due to hardware failure, and it simplifies sharing your work with clients or collaborators.

The Different Methods of Uploading Files

Drag-and-Drop via Browser

- Open your OneDrive account by logging into your Microsoft account.
- Navigate to the folder where you want to store your artwork.
- Open your computer's file explorer and select the files you want to upload.
- Drag the selected files into your OneDrive browser window. They will automatically begin uploading.

Using the Upload button

On the command bar at the top of your OneDrive page, click on **Upload**. Options to upload files or entire folders will be required.

You can add files to OneDrive in many different ways and then get to them from anywhere.

You can add files to OneDrive in many different ways and then get to them from anywhere.

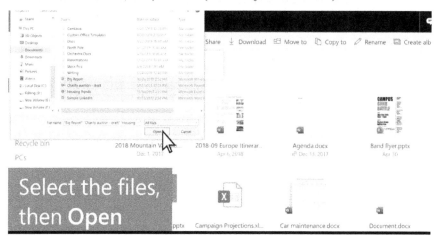

Upload from the Desktop App

- Install the OneDrive desktop application on your computer (if you haven't already).
- After installation, a OneDrive folder will appear on your computer, integrated with your file explorer.

- Simply drag your art files into this folder, and they will automatically sync to the cloud.

You can add files to OneDrive in many different ways and then get to them from anywhere.

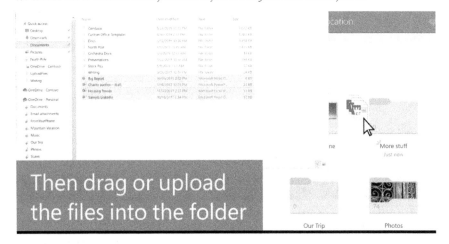

Then drag or upload the files into the folder

Using the OneDrive Mobile App

- Open the OneDrive app on your smartphone or tablet.
- Tap the **+** button (usually located at the bottom of the screen).

Tap + to...

- Choose **Upload** and select the files from your device that you wish to upload. These files will automatically sync with your OneDrive account.

Best Practices for Uploading Artwork

- **Ensure your files are well-organized before uploading**: It's easier to maintain a clean structure when you upload files into the correct folders right away.
- **Optimize file sizes when necessary**: Large artwork files can be slow to upload, so make sure the files are not unnecessarily large. Use a suitable resolution for web sharing or portfolio use without compromising the quality of your artwork.

Organizing Your Art into Folders

Once your files are uploaded to OneDrive, the next crucial step is organizing them in a way that makes sense for your portfolio. Effective organization not only helps you locate your work quickly but also enables others to navigate your portfolio with ease.

Why Organizing Is Important

A well-structured folder system will make it easier to manage your portfolio in the long term. It allows you to group your artwork based on themes, styles, dates, or any other categorization that best suits your needs. It also simplifies sharing specific pieces of artwork with clients or collaborators.

How to Organize Your Artwork

Create Folders for Major Categories

You can add files to OneDrive in many different ways and then get to them from anywhere.

You can add files to OneDrive in many different ways and then get to them from anywhere.

- For example, you can create top-level folders such as **Landscapes**, **Portraits**, **Digital Art**, or **Sketches**.

- Think of these categories as the primary themes or genres of your artwork. Every new piece should fit into one of these categories.

Subdivide Folders for Further Organization

- Inside each top-level folder, create subfolders for more specific classifications. For instance, under **Landscapes**, you could create subfolders such as **Nature** or **Cityscapes**.
- Another useful subdivision might be by the **year** or **project**, especially if you have a lot of artwork in one category.

Use Descriptive Folder Names

- Avoid vague folder names. For instance, instead of simply naming a folder "Art," try something more specific, like **2025 Exhibitions** or **Mixed Media Artwork**. This will make it easier to identify the contents at a glance.

Tips for Folder Organization

Keep the folder structure simple but logical. Don't overcomplicate it, but also avoid making it too generic.

Use a **consistent naming convention** for your folders and files. For example, you could name files with the format: **"Project Name - Date"** (e.g., "Sunset Skies - 2025"). This ensures that your files remain easy to sort.

Using Metadata & Tags for Easy Searchability

OneDrive allows you to assign metadata and tags to your files, making it easier to find and manage your artwork. Metadata is information that describes your files, such as title, artist name, or medium. Tags are keywords that you assign to your files to help describe the content.

Why Metadata & Tags Matter

When your portfolio grows over time, manually searching through folders for a specific piece can become time-consuming. By assigning metadata and tags, you can search and filter your artwork in seconds, making the process more efficient and organized.

How to Add Metadata to Your Artwork

Using File Properties in OneDrive

- Right-click on a file in your OneDrive folder and select **Properties**.
- In the **Details** tab, you can edit information like the title, artist, creation date, and more. This metadata can be helpful for distinguishing between similar pieces.

Applying Tags Directly to Files

- You can use keywords in the file's title or description that can later be used as tags.
- If you're storing a series of similar works, for example, you could use tags like **"Nature"**, **"Abstract"**, or **"Watercolor"** to quickly find specific styles or themes.

Tagging Files in OneDrive's Web Interface

OneDrive's web version allows you to add keywords or descriptive tags when uploading or organizing your files. You can add multiple tags to each file.

Use **descriptive tags** like "sunset," "illustration," or "digital painting" to group artworks based on their content or medium.

Best Practices for Metadata & Tagging

- **Be consistent with your tags**. Use a standard set of keywords that describe your work.
- **Use tags to describe the style**, medium, subject matter, and even the emotion or theme of the piece.
- Ensure that the metadata and tags accurately reflect the content of the artwork to avoid confusion.

Version History: Tracking Changes in Your Art

OneDrive's version history feature allows you to track changes made to your art files over time. This is particularly useful when you're working on a project for a long period or making revisions based on feedback.

Why Version History is Useful

If you make significant edits to a piece of art and want to compare previous versions, OneDrive's version history lets you access older versions of your files. This ensures that you can always revert to a previous draft if needed. It's also a useful feature for collaboration, as you can keep track of updates and changes made by others.

How to Use Version History

Viewing Version History

- Right-click on a file within OneDrive and select **Version History** from the menu.

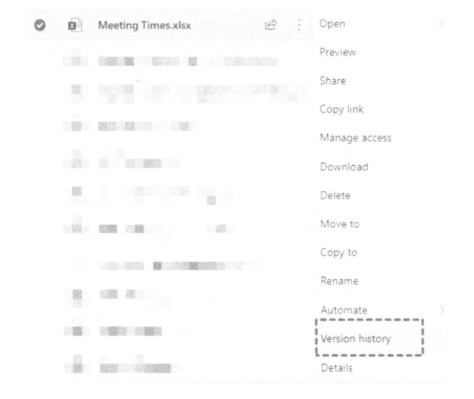

- A list of previous versions of the file will appear, showing the date and the person who made the change.

Restoring a Previous Version

- In the version history menu, select the version you want to restore.
- Click **Restore**, and the selected version will replace the current file. If you want to keep the existing file as well, you can choose to download the previous version separately.

Managing Versions of Large Files

For artwork files that undergo frequent changes (such as digital paintings or graphic designs), version history is an invaluable tool. By keeping track of these changes, you can preserve your creative process and avoid losing important revisions.

Best Practices for Using Version History

- **Name files clearly**: While version history will automatically label each version with a timestamp, giving files a clear name when you make significant changes helps to track updates more easily.
- **Review version history periodically**: If you're working on a long-term project, check your version history periodically to ensure no important revisions are lost.

By following these steps for uploading, organizing, and tracking your artwork in OneDrive, you can ensure that your portfolio remains accessible, well-structured, and easy to navigate. Implementing good habits for file management from the outset will save you time and stress as your collection grows, allowing you to focus on your creative work rather than struggling to find your files.

Part 2: Building a Digital Art Portfolio

Chapter 4: Creating a Well-Structured Portfolio

Creating a digital art portfolio is one of the most important steps an artist can take to showcase their work to potential clients, galleries, and collaborators. Whether you're an aspiring artist or a seasoned professional, having a well-structured and visually appealing portfolio is essential for making a positive impression and growing your art career. This chapter will guide you through the process of creating a digital art portfolio that stands out, from selecting the right format to structuring your collection for maximum impact.

What Makes a Great Digital Art Portfolio?

A great digital art portfolio isn't just about showing off your best pieces; it's about crafting a visual narrative that speaks to your skills, style, and creative vision. A well-thought-out portfolio helps viewers quickly understand who you are as an artist and what you bring to the table. Here are a few key elements that make a great digital portfolio:

Consistency in Style and Presentation: Your portfolio should have a consistent style that reflects your artistic identity. Whether you focus on abstract art, digital illustration, or photography, your portfolio should present a cohesive experience that speaks to your strengths.

Quality over Quantity: It's important to show your best work. A portfolio with too many pieces may overwhelm potential clients, while one with too few may fail to fully represent your skills. Aim to showcase a selection of 15-30 of your strongest pieces.

Clear Organization: A great portfolio is easy to navigate. Group related pieces together to help viewers find what they're looking for. Whether you're using OneDrive's album feature or creating a folder structure, clarity and order are key.

Diversity of Work: While consistency is important, diversity is equally crucial. Display a variety of work that shows off your technical skills, creative range, and ability to tackle different projects. This could include different mediums, styles, or subject matter.

Personal Touch: A portfolio is not just about your work—it's also about your personality as an artist. Consider adding an artist's statement or brief bio that introduces who you are, your artistic journey, and what drives your creative process.

By focusing on these key aspects, you'll create a digital art portfolio that not only showcases your skills but also tells a compelling story about your art.

Deciding on the Format: Folder-Based vs. PDF Portfolio

When it comes to choosing a format for your digital art portfolio, there are two primary options: a **folder-based portfolio** and a **PDF portfolio**. Both formats have their strengths, and the choice depends on how you intend to share and present your work.

Folder-Based Portfolio

A folder-based portfolio is essentially a collection of files and images stored in a structured folder system. It's a flexible and easily accessible format that allows you to organize your artwork in a way that is simple to update and manage.

Advantages:

- **Easy Access**: With a folder-based portfolio, clients or collaborators can easily view, download, or share specific pieces of artwork.
- **Organization Flexibility**: You can organize your portfolio by different categories, such as medium, style, or project type. This structure makes it easier for viewers to find what interests them.
- **Updates**: You can continuously update your portfolio by adding new work and removing outdated pieces without altering the entire layout.
- **Sharing**: Using cloud storage like OneDrive, you can share a folder of your portfolio with anyone via a secure link, making it accessible across multiple devices.

Disadvantages:

- **Less Control over Presentation**: While folder-based portfolios are easy to navigate, they don't offer much control over the visual layout or flow of the work.
- **Requires Viewer Interaction**: The viewer may have to sift through different folders and images to understand the full scope of your art, which could potentially lead to a less cohesive viewing experience.

PDF Portfolio

A PDF portfolio is a single file containing your artwork arranged in a layout that's tailored for presentation. This format offers more control over how your work is displayed and can be shared with ease.

Advantages:

- **Professional Presentation**: A PDF portfolio allows you to design a more polished and professional presentation of your work, with full control over layout, image placement, and text descriptions.
- **Easy Sharing**: PDF portfolios are easy to email or upload to websites. Since it's a single file, there are no issues with folder structure or broken links.
- **Sleek and Clean**: You can create a visually stunning PDF portfolio that reflects your personal aesthetic and brand.

Disadvantages:

- **Limited Flexibility**: Once you create a PDF portfolio, updating it can be more cumbersome compared to a folder-based portfolio. Adding or removing artwork requires editing the PDF.

- **File Size**: Depending on the number and resolution of your images, the PDF file can become quite large, which might make it harder to share via email or other platforms.

When choosing between a folder-based and PDF portfolio, consider your needs and how you intend to share your work. If you prefer a flexible, easily editable portfolio, a folder-based system may be right for you. If you want complete control over the presentation and prefer a more formal approach, a PDF portfolio may be the better choice.

Naming Your Files for Professionalism

File names play a significant role in maintaining professionalism and order in your digital art portfolio. Properly naming your files helps keep everything organized and easily searchable, both for you and for anyone viewing your work. Here are some tips for naming your art files:

Be Descriptive, But Concise:

- Your file names should briefly describe the artwork while avoiding overly long titles. A good format might be: [Project Title]_[Medium]_[Year]. For example, "Nature_Illustration_2022.jpg".

Use Consistent Naming Conventions:

- Consistency is key. Decide on a naming structure and stick with it across all your portfolio files. This will make it easier to search for specific pieces and maintain an organized folder system.

Avoid Special Characters and Spaces:

- When naming files, avoid using special characters (such as !, @, or #) and spaces. Use underscores or hyphens instead. This ensures that your files remain compatible with all platforms and software.

Include Your Name or Brand:

- It's a good idea to include your name or brand in each file name, especially if you're sending your portfolio to clients. For example, "JohnDoe_Portrait_2022.jpg". This adds a layer of professionalism and makes it easier to identify your work.

Date Your Work:

- Including the year or month in your file names not only helps you organize your artwork chronologically but also helps viewers understand when the piece was created, which can be especially useful if your style evolves over time.

By following these tips, you'll ensure that your digital art portfolio is not only organized but also professional-looking from the very first file.

Structuring Your Portfolio for Maximum Impact

The way you structure your digital art portfolio is crucial to how viewers perceive your work. A well-structured portfolio not only showcases your best pieces but also ensures that your artwork is presented in a way that tells a cohesive and engaging story. Here are some best practices for structuring your portfolio:

Create a Clear Introduction:

- Your portfolio should have an introduction, whether that's in the form of an artist's statement or a simple cover page. This provides context for your work and introduces viewers to your creative vision. It's also a great place to mention your artistic background, influences, and the type of work you specialize in.

Organize by Project or Theme:

- Grouping artwork by theme, project, or medium allows viewers to understand the diversity and focus of your work. For example, you could have separate sections for portrait work, landscape painting, and digital illustrations. This organization also helps viewers navigate your portfolio more easily.

Showcase Your Best Work First:

- Always place your strongest pieces at the beginning of your portfolio. This is your chance to make a great first impression, so make sure your top work is the first thing viewers see.

Tell a Story:

- Your portfolio should take the viewer on a journey. Arrange your artwork in a way that flows logically and smoothly from one piece to the next. You could tell the story of how your art has evolved over time or how different projects or series connect to one another.

Include Detailed Descriptions:

- When possible, provide brief descriptions or captions for each piece. This is particularly useful for explaining the context, inspiration, or techniques used in the artwork. A description adds value to the artwork and helps viewers connect with your creative process.

Ensure Accessibility:

- Make sure that your portfolio is easy to access and view across multiple devices. Test your OneDrive folder or PDF portfolio on various platforms to ensure it looks professional and is easy to navigate on desktop and mobile.

By following these steps, you'll be able to create a well-organized, professional, and visually engaging digital art portfolio that effectively showcases your artistic journey.

Creating a great digital art portfolio requires attention to detail, thoughtful organization, and a deep understanding of your own creative strengths. By carefully structuring your portfolio and presenting your work in the most professional way, you'll be ready to impress potential clients, collaborators, and art enthusiasts.

Chapter 5: Using OneDrive Albums to Showcase Your Art

As an artist, one of the key steps to effectively presenting your work is organizing and displaying it in a way that allows your audience to experience it in a curated, professional manner. OneDrive offers a powerful tool to help you do just that—Albums. Albums are digital collections of files, images, or other content that can be organized for easy sharing and viewing. By grouping your artwork into albums, you make it much easier for clients, potential buyers, or exhibition organizers to access and appreciate your work in the most engaging way possible.

In this chapter, we will take a detailed look at **OneDrive Albums**, why they are beneficial for artists, and how you can create and organize them to highlight your artwork effectively. You will also learn best practices for curating your albums to ensure they present your art in the most polished and professional way.

What Are OneDrive Albums?

OneDrive Albums are digital folders that allow you to group and display your files, particularly images, in a visually appealing way. These albums are not only convenient for storing your artwork, but they also provide you with the ability to showcase your art for easy sharing and viewing, either privately or publicly.

OneDrive Albums offer several advantages for artists:

- **Organization**: Albums help you keep your artwork organized in a way that makes it easier for you to find and access.
- **Collaboration**: If you're working with other artists, curators, or clients, you can share albums with specific people and control what they can see or do with the artwork.
- **Shareability**: By creating albums, you can easily share links with anyone interested in viewing your work. This is especially useful for sending your portfolio to potential clients, collectors, or exhibition curators.
- **Accessibility**: You can access your albums from any device, making it simple to update or share your work wherever you are.
- **Customization**: Each album can be customized with a title, description, and cover image, helping to give context and set the tone for the collection of artwork.

The next section will walk you through how to create and set up albums in OneDrive.

Step-by-Step Guide to Creating an Album

Creating an album on OneDrive is a simple process. By following the steps outlined below, you can quickly set up your album to organize and showcase your artwork. This process applies whether you are using OneDrive through the website or through the desktop or mobile app.

Step 1: Sign into Your OneDrive Account

- Open your browser and go to the OneDrive website or launch the OneDrive app.
- Enter your login credentials (email and password).
- Once logged in, you will be directed to your OneDrive main dashboard.

Step 2: Navigate to the Location Where You Want to Create Your Album

- From the main dashboard, go to the **"Files"** section to view your folders and documents.
- Choose the location (folder) where you want to create your album, or create a new folder if necessary.

Step 3: Start Creating the Album

- In your chosen folder, click the **"New"** button located at the top of the page.
- From the drop-down menu, select **"Album"**. This will create a new album within the folder.
- You will be prompted to name your album. Give it a descriptive title, such as the name of the art series, the theme of the collection, or the medium used.

Alternatively, follow the instructions in the screenshot below to open a new album from **Photos** on your dashboard.

1. Visit **OneDrive on the web** and sign in with your Microsoft account details.

2. Move to the **Photos** tab and select images and videos.

3. Click **Add to album** at the top.

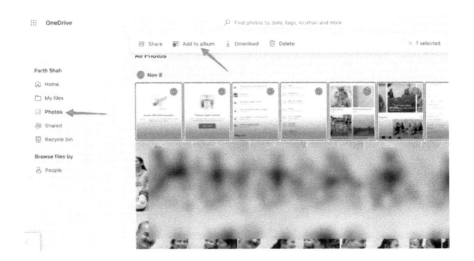

Step 4: Add Artwork to the Album

- Once your album is created, you can start adding artwork. Click on the **"Add photos and videos"** button.
- You can either drag and drop files from your computer or use the **"Browse"** option to select the files from your device.
- Select all the artwork you want to include in the album and confirm the selection. The artwork will be uploaded to the album.

Step 5: Customize the Album

- Once your artwork is uploaded, you can further customize the album by editing its details.

- Click the **"Details"** button or the album name to add a description, date, or context to the collection.
- You can also choose a **cover image** for the album to make it more visually appealing. Pick one of your artworks to serve as the album's cover or select a new image to represent the album.

Step 6: Share Your Album

- When your album is ready, you can share it with others. Click on the **"Share"** button.

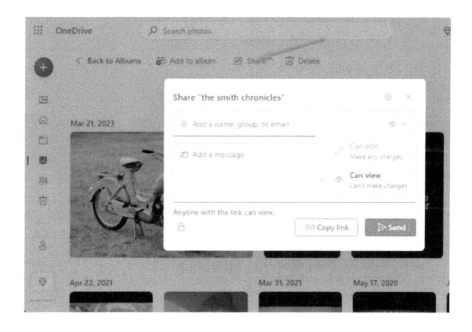

- Choose whether to send a link to the album or invite specific people to view or collaborate on the album.

- You can control the permissions, ensuring that viewers can only view the album or also have permission to edit or add comments.

Now that you know how to create an album, let's explore how to organize your artwork effectively within the album.

Organizing Artwork by Theme, Medium, or Project

A well-organized album not only makes it easier for you to manage your work but also helps your viewers experience it in a thoughtful and cohesive manner. When creating albums to showcase your artwork, it's essential to organize them in a way that makes sense for both you and your audience.

Here are some methods to consider for organizing your artwork within your albums:

1. Organizing by Theme

- **Theme-Based Organization**: Group your artwork based on common themes or concepts. For example, if you have several pieces that explore nature, you might want to create an album specifically for "Nature-Inspired Art."
- **Thematic Flow**: Ensure that the order of your artwork within the album tells a story or flows naturally. You might want to place the most striking or key pieces at the beginning to captivate your viewers.

2. Organizing by Medium

- **Medium-Specific Albums**: If you work in different artistic mediums (e.g., digital painting, watercolor, sculpture), you can create separate albums for each. This makes it easier for potential buyers or curators to view your work based on their specific interests or the medium they prefer.
- **Medium Comparison**: Consider grouping related artworks that show your evolution within a specific medium. This could help demonstrate your versatility and skill in different artistic styles.

3. Organizing by Project or Series

- **Project-Based Organization**: If you work on multiple projects or collections, create albums for each project or series of artwork. For example, if you've worked on a specific art series for an exhibition, dedicate an album to that particular collection.
- **Chronological Order**: Within each project or series, you may want to arrange the artworks in chronological order to show the progression or development of your work over time.

The key here is to consider your audience. For instance, a potential buyer or curator might want to see a specific style or medium. Organizing your albums in a thoughtful, accessible way will help them find exactly what they're looking for.

Best Practices for Curating a Professional Portfolio

Your OneDrive albums serve as a powerful tool for showcasing your artwork to the world. However, the way you curate and present your albums can make a significant difference in how your work is perceived. Here are some best practices to ensure that your digital portfolio reflects your professionalism and artistic vision.

1. Keep Your Portfolio Focused and Cohesive

- **Limit the Number of Pieces**: Choose only your best and most representative work for each album. It's better to have a smaller, high-quality selection than to overwhelm your audience with too many pieces.
- **Maintain Consistency**: Each album should convey a clear sense of unity. Avoid including too many disparate pieces unless they serve a clear purpose or tell a cohesive story.

2. Provide Context and Descriptions

- **Include Descriptions for Each Piece**: A brief description for each artwork can provide context and help the viewer understand your creative process. Explain the inspiration behind the work, any challenges you faced, or the techniques used.
- **Include Titles, Mediums, and Dimensions**: Make sure to provide relevant details such as the title of the piece, the medium used, and the dimensions (if applicable). This information is essential for collectors, curators, and clients who might want to learn more about your work.

3. Pay Attention to Visual Presentation

- **Thumbnail Images**: Ensure that your album's thumbnail images look professional. Avoid using blurry or low-quality images as your cover photo or album thumbnail.
- **Image Quality**: Ensure that all images are of high resolution, clear, and properly lit. Your viewers should be able to appreciate the fine details of your work.

4. Organize and Update Regularly

- **Keep Your Portfolio Fresh**: Regularly update your albums with new pieces and remove older works that no longer represent your current style or artistic direction.
- **Review and Edit**: Periodically review your albums to ensure that they still reflect your best work. Curate with purpose and keep your portfolio aligned with your artistic goals.

By following these best practices, you'll ensure that your OneDrive albums serve as powerful tools for showcasing your art and leaving a lasting impression on your audience.

Chapter 6: Editing and Enhancing Images in OneDrive

OneDrive is not only a cloud storage solution, but it also provides some basic yet powerful tools to help you manage and enhance your digital artwork. While OneDrive may not offer the advanced capabilities of professional image editing software like Photoshop, it provides essential editing features that can help you make quick adjustments to your files without leaving the platform. In this chapter, we will walk through the basics of image editing in OneDrive, explore third-party integrations for more advanced tasks, and discuss how to optimize images for online viewing.

With OneDrive's editing tools, artists can crop, resize, and adjust their images in a simple, user-friendly interface. These tools are useful when you need to make basic adjustments before sharing or displaying your artwork. Let's start by exploring the basic image editing features in OneDrive.

Basic Image Editing Tools in OneDrive

OneDrive offers several built-in image editing tools that can help you make quick improvements to your artwork. These tools are accessible directly from the OneDrive interface, which means you can edit your images without having to leave the platform. The available editing options are designed for simplicity and efficiency.

The most common basic image editing features in OneDrive include:

- **Cropping**: Crop images to focus on specific parts of your artwork.

- **Resizing**: Resize your images to fit specific dimensions or to reduce file sizes for faster sharing.
- **Adjusting Brightness and Contrast**: Fine-tune the brightness and contrast of your images to enhance visibility and improve clarity.
- **Rotating**: Rotate your images to the desired orientation.
- **Filters**: Apply simple filters to enhance or modify the color tone of your images.

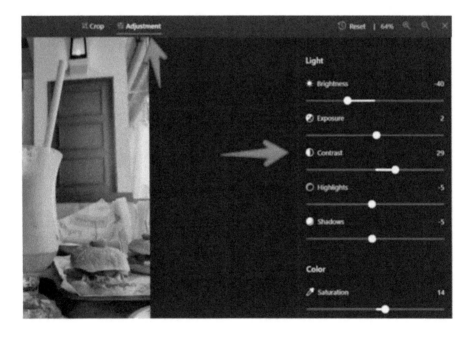

To use the basic editing tools, you need to first open the image in OneDrive's preview mode. After that, you can access the editing options by selecting the "Edit" button, which will provide a toolbar with available features. These tools are easy to use and do not require extensive editing skills, making them perfect for artists who want to quickly improve their digital artwork.

Let's take a deeper look at some of the most important editing options.

Resizing, Cropping, and Adjusting Brightness

Once you've accessed the image editing tools in OneDrive, you can begin making adjustments to your images. The following sections explain each of these features in detail.

Resizing Your Image

Resizing is one of the most commonly used editing features in OneDrive. It allows you to adjust the dimensions of an image to fit specific requirements, whether you're preparing your portfolio for web display, printing, or sending it to clients.

Steps for resizing an image:

- **Open the image**: Double-click the image file to open it in the OneDrive preview.
- **Click on "Edit"**: Once the image is open, select the "Edit" button.
- **Select the resize option**: From the editing toolbar, choose the resize feature.
- **Adjust the dimensions**: You can adjust the width and height of the image manually, or you can set it to a specific size (e.g., 1024 x 768 pixels).

- **Save the changes**: After resizing the image, don't forget to save your work.

Resizing can also help in reducing the file size, which is particularly useful for online sharing. A smaller image file size ensures quicker load times when viewed on websites or social media platforms.

Cropping Your Image

Cropping is another essential image editing function that allows you to remove unwanted areas of your artwork and focus attention on the most important parts. This is particularly useful if you want to emphasize certain details in your art or if you need to trim the borders.

Steps for cropping an image:

- **Open the image** in OneDrive's preview mode.
- **Click on "Edit"** to access the editing tools.
- **Select the crop tool** from the toolbar.
- **Adjust the crop area**: Drag the corners or sides of the cropping tool to adjust the area you want to keep. Anything outside of the selected area will be cropped out.
- **Apply the crop**: Once you're satisfied with the cropped area, apply the crop to finalize your changes.
- **Save your work**: Don't forget to save the image after cropping.

Cropping helps improve the composition of your artwork and can make the subject of the image stand out more clearly.

Adjusting Brightness and Contrast

Adjusting the brightness and contrast of an image can significantly enhance its visual appeal. Brightness controls how light or dark the image appears, while contrast adjusts the difference between the light and dark areas of the image.

Steps for adjusting brightness and contrast:

- **Open the image** in the OneDrive preview mode.
- **Click "Edit"** to access the editing options.
- **Select the "Brightness/Contrast" slider** from the toolbar.
- **Adjust the brightness**: Slide the brightness control left to darken the image or right to lighten it.
- **Adjust the contrast**: Slide the contrast control left to reduce contrast or right to increase the difference between light and dark areas.
- **Preview the changes**: As you adjust the sliders, you can see the real-time effect of the changes.
- **Save the adjustments**: Once you are happy with the adjustments, save your image.

Brightness and contrast adjustments are useful for making your artwork more vibrant or for ensuring that key details are not too dark or overexposed.

Third-Party Integrations for Advanced Editing

While OneDrive offers basic editing features, you may find that you need more advanced tools for tasks like retouching, adding special effects, or working with multiple layers. Fortunately, OneDrive integrates with third-party applications, such as Adobe Photoshop, GIMP, and others, to provide enhanced editing capabilities.

By linking OneDrive with these applications, you can:

- **Access your images directly** from OneDrive without downloading them.
- **Edit in advanced software** that offers a broader range of tools and features.
- **Save edited images back to OneDrive**, ensuring all your work remains in one place.

For example, you can open an image from OneDrive in Photoshop, use advanced filters, adjustments, and retouching tools, and then save the enhanced image back to OneDrive. This allows you to combine the convenience of cloud storage with the power of professional editing software.

To integrate third-party tools with OneDrive:

- **Link your OneDrive account** with the third-party application (such as Adobe Photoshop).
- **Open the image from OneDrive** directly within the third-party app.
- **Edit the image** as you normally would in the external software.
- **Save and sync** the edited image back to OneDrive.

These integrations are perfect for artists who need professional-level editing without leaving the cloud environment.

Optimizing Images for Online Viewing

After editing your images, it's important to optimize them for online viewing. Optimizing images involves adjusting them so they look their best on websites, social media, and other digital platforms, while also ensuring that the file size is small enough for fast loading times.

Here are some steps to optimize your images:

- **Resize the image to fit the required dimensions** for the platform you plan to use. For instance, social media platforms often have recommended image sizes, such as 1200 x 800 pixels for Facebook.
- **Reduce the file size**: Large image files can slow down webpage load times. Use OneDrive's resize tool or an external editing application to compress the image without losing quality.
- **Choose the right file format**: For online use, JPEGs and PNGs are commonly used. JPEGs are great for photos and complex images, while PNGs work well for images with transparency.
- **Enhance the visual quality**: Adjust the brightness, contrast, and sharpness to ensure that the image appears clear and vibrant on digital screens.

By optimizing your images, you ensure that your artwork is displayed properly across all digital platforms and that viewers have a seamless experience.

Conclusion

Editing and enhancing images in OneDrive can be incredibly useful for artists who need to make quick adjustments to their work before sharing it with clients or displaying it online. From basic cropping and resizing to more advanced editing with third-party integrations, OneDrive provides everything you need to manage and present your art in a polished, professional manner.

Always remember to optimize your images for online viewing by adjusting the file size, format, and visual elements to ensure your portfolio looks its best on any platform. By following the steps outlined in this chapter, you'll be able to efficiently edit and enhance your digital artwork while keeping everything organized and backed up in OneDrive.

Part 3: Sharing and Presenting Your Portfolio

Chapter 7: Sharing Your Portfolio with Clients & Galleries

Sharing your digital portfolio is one of the most essential steps in showcasing your work to potential clients, collaborators, and galleries. OneDrive offers several robust features to help you securely share your artwork while controlling who can view, comment on, or edit your work. By mastering the tools available, you can ensure that your artwork is presented professionally, with the right level of access for different audiences. In this chapter, we will walk through the process of generating shareable links, setting permissions, and distributing your portfolio in various ways, all while maintaining a high level of control over your content.

How to Generate Shareable Links

Generating shareable links is one of the simplest and most effective ways to present your portfolio to others. Whether you are sharing individual pieces of artwork or entire collections, the process is straightforward and quick. When you create a shareable link in OneDrive, you are essentially allowing someone to access your file or folder remotely, without needing to send physical copies of your work.

Why Generate Shareable Links?

- **Easy Access:** Clients, potential buyers, or galleries can view your work without needing to download large files or worry about compatibility.
- **Convenience:** You can create a single link for an entire folder, making it easier to share multiple pieces at once.
- **Control:** You can manage access permissions and track who views your artwork.

Steps to Generate a Shareable Link

- **Log in to OneDrive:** First, sign in to your OneDrive account through your browser or the desktop app.
- **Locate the Portfolio Folder or File:** Find the folder or specific artwork that you want to share. You can do this by navigating to the relevant directory where your files are stored.
- **Select the File or Folder:** Click on the file or folder to highlight it.
- **Click the Share Button:** In the OneDrive interface, there will be a "Share" option available once you have selected the file or folder. This can be found either in the toolbar at the top or by right-clicking the file.

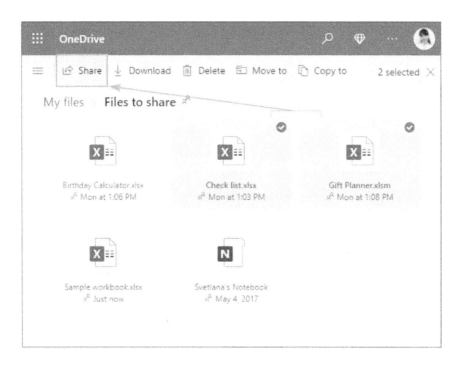

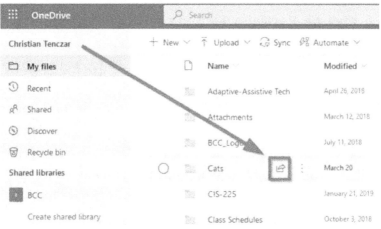

Using the share icon beside the file or folder

- **Choose Link Settings:** You will be prompted with several sharing options. Select the option that best suits your needs (e.g., anyone with the link, people in your organization, or specific people).

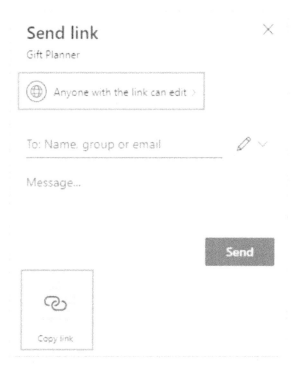

- **Copy the Link:** After adjusting the settings, OneDrive will generate a link that you can copy to your clipboard. You can now send this link to your clients, galleries, or other viewers.

The link you generate will give recipients access to view the files or folders you shared. Depending on your permission settings, you can restrict access to only viewing or allow edits.

Setting Access Permissions (View-Only vs. Editable Links)

OneDrive gives you the flexibility to control what your recipients can do with your artwork once they receive the link. You can create **view-only links** or **editable links**, depending on whether you want them to simply view your portfolio or make changes to it.

View-Only Links

This option is the most common for showcasing your portfolio. It ensures that recipients can only view your files and cannot make any changes to them. View-only links are ideal when you are sharing your work with clients, galleries, or other artists for feedback without risking accidental edits or deletions.

When to Use: Ideal when you want to showcase your work or share it for evaluation, but not for editing.

How to Set View-Only Permissions:

- After generating the shareable link (as described in the previous section), choose the **"Anyone with the link can view"** option.

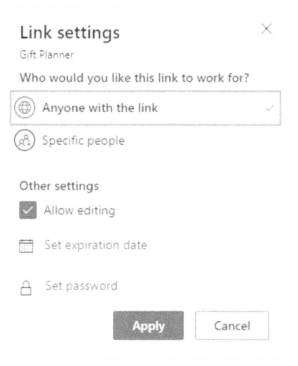

- Ensure that the **"Allow editing"** box is unchecked.
- Click **"Apply"** to finalize the settings.

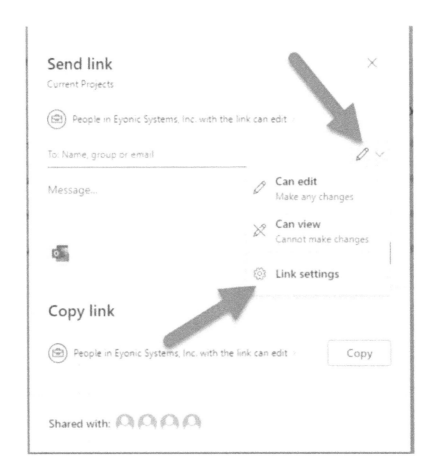

Editable Links

If you are collaborating with someone, such as a client requesting changes to a specific piece or a gallery needing to make adjustments to the description of your work, you can provide them with editable links. This allows them to make changes to your files, whether that means leaving comments, uploading files, or even editing existing artwork (if you've given them the ability to do so).

When to Use: Ideal when you are working on collaborative projects or when you need a client or gallery to provide direct feedback or revisions.

How to Set Editable Permissions:

- After generating the shareable link, ensure that the **"Allow editing"** box is checked.
- This will allow recipients to make changes to your portfolio files, such as adding comments or uploading new versions of artwork.

Creating Private vs. Public Portfolio Links

When sharing your portfolio, it is important to understand the difference between **private** and **public** links. Public links are accessible by anyone with the link, which can be useful for general distribution, such as sending your portfolio to a large audience. However, if you want to restrict access to specific people, you can create private links.

Private Portfolio Links

Private links allow you to control exactly who can access your portfolio. You can choose specific individuals, such as potential clients or gallery owners, and provide them with the link. These links require a person to enter their email or sign in with a Microsoft account, ensuring that only authorized viewers can access your work.

When to Use: Ideal for sensitive or high-value artwork, when you want to maintain a tight grip on who sees your work.

How to Create a Private Link:

After selecting **"Specific people"** in the link-sharing options, input the email addresses of the people you wish to share your portfolio with.

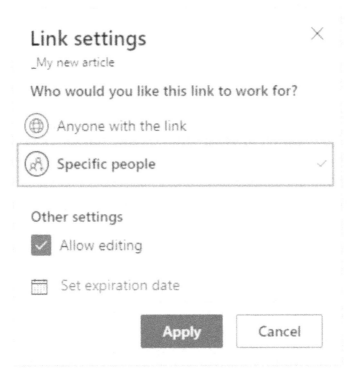

You can also require the recipients to sign in with their Microsoft account to verify their identity before accessing the portfolio.

Public Portfolio Links

Public links, on the other hand, are perfect for more general or open sharing. Anyone with the link can access your portfolio, even if they don't have a OneDrive or Microsoft account. This is beneficial when you want to share your portfolio broadly, such as when you are applying for public exhibitions or submitting work for online competitions.

When to Use: Ideal for wider distribution, especially when there are no security concerns or if you want to make your portfolio easily accessible.

How to Create a Public Link:

After selecting **"Anyone with the link"** in the sharing options, you can choose to allow the link to be forwarded, making your portfolio publicly accessible.

You can also disable the option for editing or adding comments, ensuring that your portfolio remains static.

Sending Portfolios via Email or Social Media

Once you've generated your shareable link and decided on the appropriate permissions (view-only or editable, private or public), the next step is to distribute your portfolio. OneDrive makes it simple to send your portfolio directly via email or through various social media platforms, allowing you to reach clients and galleries wherever they are.

Sending via Email

Email is one of the most professional ways to send your portfolio link to clients or galleries. It ensures that your portfolio reaches the right person, and you can include a personalized message along with the link.

How to Send via Email:

- Open your email application and create a new message.
- Include a subject line such as **"My Digital Art Portfolio for Review"** or **"Portfolio Submission for Gallery Exhibition"**.
- Paste the shareable link into the body of the email. You can also add a brief introduction or explanation of your work, highlighting specific pieces that you want the recipient to focus on.
- Send the email to the intended recipient(s).

Sending via Social Media

Social media is another great avenue for showcasing your work and engaging with a larger audience. If you have a professional social media presence (such as LinkedIn, Instagram, or Facebook), you can easily share your OneDrive portfolio link directly through these platforms.

How to Send via Social Media:

- Copy the shareable link from OneDrive.

- Paste it into a post, message, or comment on your social media account.
- Add relevant hashtags, descriptions, or tags to make your post discoverable to your followers and potential clients or galleries.

By following these steps, you can confidently share your digital art portfolio with the world, while maintaining control over how your artwork is viewed and interacted with. The flexibility of OneDrive allows you to adapt your sharing methods to fit the needs of your clients and collaborators, ensuring a seamless and professional experience for everyone involved.

Chapter 8: Presenting Your Art Portfolio Online

In today's digital age, having an online presence is essential for any artist. OneDrive offers multiple ways for you to share and display your art portfolio, making it easily accessible to clients, fans, and potential buyers. This chapter will guide you through the process of presenting your art portfolio online, including how to embed OneDrive files on your website or blog, use OneDrive to host a portfolio on social media platforms like Instagram and LinkedIn, and integrate OneDrive with digital resumes and online art marketplaces.

By the end of this chapter, you'll have a clear understanding of how to enhance your digital presence and ensure that your art is seen by the right audience. Each section will walk you through the various options for sharing your work and the steps involved in utilizing OneDrive as an effective portfolio-hosting tool.

Embedding OneDrive Files on Your Website or Blog

Many artists today use websites or blogs as a primary platform for showcasing their portfolios. OneDrive makes it simple to embed your digital art files directly on your site, ensuring that your work is available for viewing without visitors needing to download anything. By embedding your OneDrive files, you can create a seamless experience for your audience.

Before embedding, it's important to understand what the embedding process entails. Embedding is the act of placing a link or a preview of your file directly into the code of your website. This enables visitors to view your art within the context of your website or blog page, without having to navigate away.

Steps to Embed OneDrive Files on Your Website or Blog:

Upload the Art Files to OneDrive:

- Begin by uploading your artwork to OneDrive. Ensure that your files are organized within folders or albums, making it easier to find the specific files you wish to embed.
- Uploading art in high-quality formats (such as JPEG or PNG) will ensure that your work appears crisp and clear when embedded.

Set Permissions for File Sharing:

- Before embedding, you need to share the file publicly or with specific people.

- To do this, right-click the file or folder in OneDrive and select "Share." Choose "Anyone with the link" to allow for easy embedding, and set the permissions to "Can view" (which will allow viewers to see the file without altering it).

Get the Embed Code:

- After you've set the permissions, click on the "Copy Link" button to get a shareable URL.
- If your website allows for embedding, OneDrive provides an "Embed" option under the sharing settings. This will give you an HTML code that can be placed directly into your website's content.

Place the Embed Code in Your Website's HTML:

- Copy the HTML code that OneDrive provides. Open your website's content management system (CMS), like WordPress, and paste the code into the area where you want your art to appear.
- For blogs, you can simply paste the code into a post's HTML editor, ensuring that your portfolio image appears within the blog post.

Preview and Publish:

- Once you've added the embed code, preview the page to see how your artwork appears. Make any necessary adjustments to the layout.

- When satisfied, publish the page to showcase your artwork to your visitors.

Using OneDrive to Host a Portfolio for Instagram or LinkedIn

Social media platforms such as Instagram and LinkedIn are excellent tools for showcasing your art and reaching a broader audience. While Instagram focuses heavily on visual content, LinkedIn allows for more professional networking. Both platforms offer unique ways to share your art portfolio, and OneDrive can play a key role in hosting your artwork for easy access.

Steps to Use OneDrive for Social Media Portfolios:

Upload Your Portfolio Files to OneDrive:

- Start by uploading all the artworks you want to feature on Instagram or LinkedIn. You can organize these files in a OneDrive folder, ensuring that they're easy to access and share.
- If you plan to use the portfolio for multiple platforms, consider creating specific albums tailored to each platform's audience.

Generate Shareable Links:

- Once the files are uploaded, generate shareable links for each artwork or album you want to share. Right-click the file in OneDrive, select "Share," and choose "Anyone with the link" for easy sharing.
- Copy the link provided. This link will be used to share your art via Instagram, LinkedIn, or other platforms.

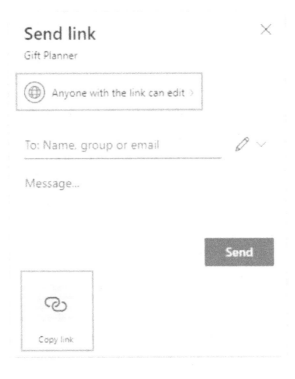

Share on Instagram (Using Stories or Bio Links):

- Instagram doesn't allow for direct embedding of OneDrive links in posts. However, you can add your portfolio link to your Instagram bio. In your bio section, add a call-to-action like "View my full portfolio at" followed by your OneDrive link.

- For Instagram Stories, use the "Link" sticker to share a link to your OneDrive album or specific artwork.

Share on LinkedIn (Using Posts or Profile Section):

- For LinkedIn, you can directly share your artwork in posts. Paste your OneDrive link into the post caption, and it will display a preview of your portfolio or specific artwork.
- Additionally, consider adding your OneDrive portfolio link to your LinkedIn profile in the "Featured" section, where people can easily view your work.

Monitor Engagement and Update Regularly:

- Keep track of the interactions your posts receive. LinkedIn allows you to engage with professionals, while Instagram gives you instant feedback from a broader audience.
- Update your portfolio regularly, ensuring that you have fresh work to share, keeping your audience engaged.

Integrating OneDrive with Digital Resumes & Online Art Marketplaces

As an artist, presenting a polished digital resume and using online art marketplaces can significantly improve your visibility and chances of landing commissions or sales. OneDrive can help you integrate your portfolio into these platforms, making it simple for clients, art buyers, and employers to access and evaluate your work.

Steps to Integrate OneDrive with Digital Resumes and Marketplaces:

Create a Digital Resume with Portfolio Links:

- Start by creating a digital version of your resume using tools like Google Docs, Microsoft Word, or even PDF editors.
- In your resume, include direct links to your OneDrive portfolio, highlighting specific works that match the job description or project you're applying for. Use text like "View my portfolio on OneDrive" and hyperlink it to your art folder.
- Be sure to use an attractive layout that reflects your artistic style while maintaining professionalism.

Incorporate OneDrive in Online Art Marketplaces:

- Many art marketplaces, such as Etsy or Saatchi Art, allow you to showcase your work directly on their platform. However, if you have a large collection or want to maintain an up-to-date portfolio, consider linking to your OneDrive gallery from your marketplace profile.
- Similar to LinkedIn or Instagram, you can copy the OneDrive shareable link and include it in your marketplace profile description, allowing potential buyers or clients to explore your full range of work.

Make Your Portfolio Accessible from Your Resume or Website:

- If you're submitting your resume to clients or galleries, or if you have your website set up, make sure that your OneDrive portfolio is easily accessible. Add a clickable link to your portfolio that is clearly visible in the header, footer, or contact section of your digital resume or website.

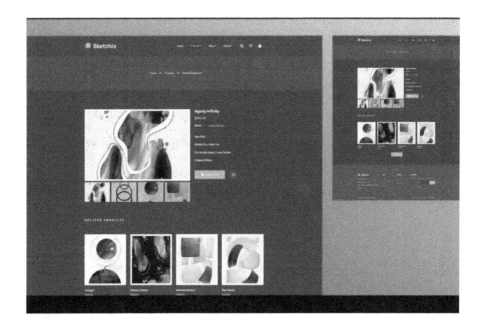

Maintain Up-to-Date Artworks Across All Platforms:

- Consistency is key when showcasing your art across various online platforms. Regularly update your OneDrive portfolio and ensure that these updates reflect across your digital resume, LinkedIn, Instagram, and art marketplaces.
- If your artwork evolves over time, make sure that you're continually adding new pieces to your portfolio so your audience sees the latest and best of your work.

By embedding OneDrive files, hosting your portfolio on social media platforms, and integrating OneDrive with digital resumes and online art marketplaces, you are effectively positioning yourself as a professional artist in the digital space. Remember, sharing and presenting your art portfolio is not just about uploading your work—it's about creating a digital experience that engages your audience, whether they're potential clients, art buyers, or collaborators.

With these tools and techniques, you can make your artwork more accessible, ensure it reaches a wider audience, and showcase your creativity to the world.

Chapter 9: Collaborating with Clients, Teams, and Art Collectors

Collaborating with others is an essential part of being an artist, especially in today's connected world. Whether you are working with a team of co-creators, receiving feedback from clients, or collaborating with galleries and art consultants, efficient collaboration ensures your artwork reaches its full potential. OneDrive offers numerous tools and features to help streamline this process, making it easier to work together on digital portfolios, share artwork, and manage revisions. In this chapter, we'll explore how to use OneDrive to facilitate collaboration with clients, co-creators, and collectors, and how to manage art commissions and revisions efficiently.

How to Allow Feedback and Comments on Your Artwork

Feedback is vital to an artist's growth. OneDrive makes it easy to receive and manage feedback on your artwork, whether it's from clients, team members, or collaborators. Here's how to allow others to comment on your artwork.

- **Choose the Right Folder or File**
  First, you need to select the artwork or the folder containing the artwork you wish to share for feedback. If you're working on a group of images, it's best to upload them into a shared folder rather than sharing individual files, as this will allow for easier access and organization.

Set the Sharing Permissions

- To allow others to comment on your files, open OneDrive, find your artwork folder or file, and click on the "Share" button.
- In the sharing options, choose "Anyone with the link can edit" or "Specific people" and enter their email addresses. Ensure that the "Allow editing" option is checked. This will give them the ability to add comments directly on the artwork.
- OneDrive also gives you the flexibility to set whether people can view or edit the content, so you can keep control of the artwork while allowing others to leave feedback.

Communicate Expectations Clearly

- Before sharing the file, clearly communicate what kind of feedback you are looking for. For example, you may want input on specific aspects like color composition, overall design, or theme. By providing specific instructions, you can ensure the feedback you receive is relevant and helpful.

Access Comments and Track Changes

- As feedback is left on your artwork, you'll be notified by email. To view and respond to comments, simply open the file in OneDrive.
- Comments will be visible in the margin of the file, and you can respond directly to each comment to keep a running dialogue with your collaborators.
- If multiple people are commenting on a piece of artwork, you can use the @mention feature to tag specific people, making sure everyone knows when a comment is directed at them.

Incorporate Feedback

- After reviewing all the feedback, you can make changes to your artwork as necessary. Since OneDrive automatically saves previous versions, you can revert to earlier versions if needed, which ensures that you don't lose any important work.

Real-Time Collaboration with Teams and Co-Creators

Real-time collaboration has become a key aspect of many art projects. Whether you are creating a joint piece of artwork with a co-creator or working with a team on a series of designs, OneDrive allows you to collaborate in real-time. This is particularly useful for projects that require quick decisions and immediate updates.

Set Up a Shared Folder or File

- Begin by creating a shared folder for the project. Within this folder, you can upload all related files—whether they are digital sketches, finished pieces, drafts, or reference materials. Make sure all contributors have access to the folder by selecting "Share" and entering their email addresses. You can also invite people via a link.

Edit Simultaneously

- OneDrive allows you and your co-creators to edit the artwork simultaneously in real-time. When a team member edits the artwork, changes will appear immediately, and you will see who made the edits. This live collaboration feature ensures that you can see adjustments as they happen, which can speed up the creative process.

Version History and Comments

- As edits are made, OneDrive automatically saves versions of your files. If you're collaborating with multiple people, this can be invaluable, as it allows you to keep track of all the changes and roll back to previous versions if necessary.
- At any point during the collaboration, team members can leave comments on the artwork to discuss changes, suggest new ideas, or ask questions. This feature helps keep everyone on the same page, especially when working on larger projects that involve several contributors.

Organize Collaboration Tasks

- If you have a large team working on different aspects of the project (for example, one person handles backgrounds while another focuses on characters), use OneDrive's folder structure to keep everything organized. Create subfolders for each stage of the project or different tasks. You can also create separate folders for drafts, finished work, and feedback so everything is neatly divided.

Real-Time Communication

- For smoother communication, it's a good idea to use OneDrive in tandem with a communication platform like Microsoft Teams or Skype. These tools integrate seamlessly with OneDrive and allow you to chat in real time, share updates, and discuss changes as you work.

Working with Galleries and Art Consultants Using OneDrive

When you're ready to share your portfolio with galleries, art consultants, or potential buyers, OneDrive becomes an invaluable tool. It makes sharing high-quality images easy, while giving you full control over permissions and access.

Creating a Portfolio for Galleries or Art Consultants

- Start by organizing your artwork into a digital portfolio within a dedicated folder in OneDrive. Create a separate folder for each collection or theme, or organize your artwork based on size, medium, or style.

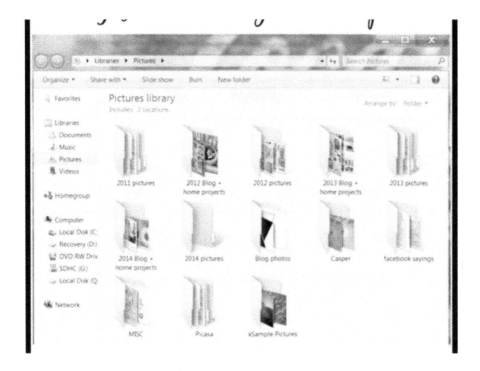

- If you are working with multiple galleries or consultants, it might be helpful to create personalized folders for each client.

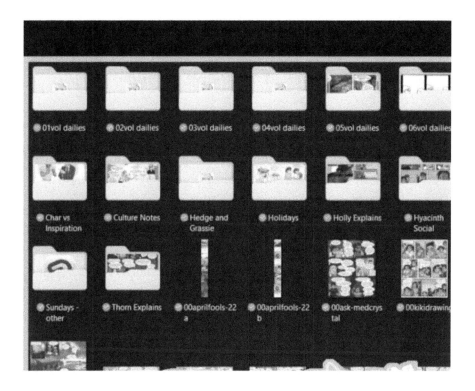

Sending Files to Galleries

- When sharing your portfolio with a gallery, you can either send a direct link to the OneDrive folder or use the "Share" button to send an email invitation. Be sure to choose the correct permission settings: for galleries, it's often best to set the permissions to "view only" so that your work is protected.

Customizing Permissions

- OneDrive allows you to adjust permissions so that galleries or consultants can only view the artwork without downloading or editing it. If you need to collaborate on revisions or discuss specific pieces, you can grant them "editing" access temporarily.

Setting Up Secure Payment and Delivery Options

- If you are working with art collectors or clients who wish to purchase artwork, OneDrive offers a secure way to deliver high-resolution images. After finalizing a sale or agreement, you can share high-quality versions of your artwork while keeping other files secure.

Tracking Portfolio Views

- OneDrive can be used to monitor who has accessed your portfolio by using the "Activity" feature. This can give you insights into which pieces are getting the most attention, which may help you prioritize follow-ups with clients or galleries.

Managing Art Commissions and Client Revisions

When working on commissioned art pieces, managing revisions and client feedback can be challenging, especially if the client is providing extensive feedback over time. OneDrive offers several features to make this process easier, ensuring smooth communication and efficient handling of revisions.

Organizing Commissioned Artwork

- Create a dedicated folder for each commissioned project to keep everything organized. Within the folder, you can store contracts, reference materials, drafts, and the final artwork. This will help both you and your clients stay on track throughout the project.

Receiving and Tracking Client Revisions

- Once the initial draft of the commissioned artwork is complete, share it with your client using OneDrive's sharing features. They can leave comments and feedback directly on the file. You can use these comments to guide your revisions and track changes over time.

Version Control and Client Approval

- OneDrive's version history feature allows you to keep track of revisions made to artwork. If a client requests a change or revision, you can make edits and save new versions while preserving the original. This makes it easy to keep track of changes and show clients the progression of the artwork.

Finalizing Artwork and Delivering to Clients

- After revisions are complete and the client has approved the final piece, you can share the high-resolution file with them via OneDrive. If needed, you can also include a PDF invoice or other documents related to the commission. By using OneDrive's sharing features, you can ensure a smooth, secure delivery process for both parties.

Archiving Completed Projects

- After the project is finished, you may want to archive it for future reference or portfolio use. OneDrive allows you to store completed commissions in a way that's easy to access later, whether you want to revisit the project for personal reference or showcase it in your portfolio.

By utilizing OneDrive's features for collaboration, feedback, and project management, you can streamline the entire process of working with clients, teams, galleries, and art consultants. This not only saves time but also enhances the professionalism and organization of your artistic business. Whether you're receiving feedback, managing revisions, or working on commissions, OneDrive offers a centralized platform that keeps your workflow efficient and your creative process on track.

Part 4: Security, Backup, and Portfolio Maintenance

Chapter 10: Protecting Your Art from Unauthorized Use

As an artist, safeguarding your work in the digital realm is a crucial part of maintaining your intellectual property rights and ensuring that your creations are not misused. With the growth of the internet and online platforms, sharing your art digitally has become easier, but it has also made it more vulnerable to unauthorized use and theft. In this chapter, we will discuss various strategies and tools available in OneDrive to protect your art, including setting access permissions, preventing unauthorized downloads, using watermarks, and understanding copyright laws.

Setting File Access Permissions Correctly

One of the most effective ways to protect your art stored in OneDrive is by configuring file access permissions. By doing so, you control who can see, download, and edit your files. OneDrive gives you flexibility in managing access, making it an essential tool for keeping your art secure.

Before diving into specific permission settings, it's essential to understand the two main types of access you can assign:

- **View-only Access**: This allows users to only view the files or artwork you've shared. They cannot make any changes or download the file.
- **Edit Access**: This grants the user permission to modify the file, upload new versions, or make other changes. However, this level of access should be granted with caution.

Steps to Set File Access Permissions in OneDrive:

- **Log in to Your OneDrive Account**: Open OneDrive on your computer or mobile device, and log in with your Microsoft account.
- **Select the File or Folder**: Navigate to the artwork or folder you wish to protect. Click on the file or folder to highlight it.
- **Click on the "Share" Button**: This button is usually located at the top of the screen. Clicking it will open the sharing options.
- **Choose the Permission Level**:
    - For **view-only access**, select "Can view" under the sharing options.
    - For **edit access**, choose "Can edit."
- **Choose Who Can Access the File**: You can either:
    - Share with **specific people** by entering their email addresses.
    - Share with **anyone with the link** (be cautious with this option, as it opens up your art to broader access).
- **Set Expiration Dates (Optional)**: For additional security, OneDrive allows you to set an expiration date on the link,

meaning the recipient will no longer have access after that date.

- **Send the Invitation**: Once you've set the desired permissions, click "Send" to share your artwork with the specified individuals.

By controlling access at this level, you can ensure that only authorized individuals can view or interact with your artwork.

How to Prevent Unauthorized Downloads

One of the primary concerns for digital artists is preventing their artwork from being downloaded or distributed without their permission. While OneDrive cannot fully guarantee that someone won't capture your work using third-party tools (such as screenshots), it does provide several features to minimize the risk of unauthorized downloading.

Steps to Prevent Unauthorized Downloads:

Use View-Only Permissions:

- As mentioned earlier, ensuring that recipients only have "view-only" access is one of the simplest and most effective ways to prevent unauthorized downloads.
- With **view-only access**, users can view the artwork but cannot download or copy it.

Disable Downloading for Shared Links:

- When sharing your artwork via OneDrive, you can disable the download option altogether. This feature ensures that recipients can only view your files in their browser without downloading them.
- To disable downloading, when sharing your file, click the "Anyone with the link" option.
- Then, click the "Link settings" and toggle off the "Allow editing" and "Allow download" options.

Utilize a Secure Web Viewer:

- You can also opt to use a secure online viewer for your artwork, such as a PDF viewer or image viewer that limits downloading. This restricts users to only viewing the content without the ability to download or copy it directly.

Add a Custom Watermark (to be discussed next):

- A visible watermark can act as a deterrent against unauthorized downloads and use by displaying your brand or copyright information.

Using Watermarks for Online Portfolios

Watermarks are a simple yet effective way to protect your art from unauthorized use, especially in the digital world. A watermark is typically a semi-transparent logo or text placed over your artwork. It serves two primary purposes:

- **Deterrence**: It makes it harder for people to steal your art or use it without proper credit.
- **Identification**: It makes your artwork easily traceable back to you as the creator.

While watermarks are not foolproof (as they can be removed by skilled individuals), they significantly reduce the chances of theft, especially when your art is displayed publicly or shared online.

Steps to Add a Watermark to Your Artwork:

- **Select the Artwork to Watermark**: Choose the digital file (e.g., image or PDF) you wish to protect by adding a watermark.
- **Choose a Watermark Tool**: You can use various software tools for adding watermarks, such as Adobe Photoshop, GIMP, or even online tools like Canva.

Create Your Watermark:

- **Logo Watermark**: If you have a personal logo, you can add it as a watermark.
- **Text Watermark**: If you don't have a logo, consider adding your name or a copyright statement as text.
- **Place the Watermark on the Artwork**: Position the watermark in a place that does not obscure the artwork but is still noticeable (e.g., in the corner or across the center).
- **Adjust the Transparency**: Make sure the watermark is semi-transparent so that it does not overpower the artwork itself but remains visible enough to deter theft.

- **Save the Watermarked File**: Once the watermark is added, save the file with the watermark applied. This version is now ready for online sharing or public display.

By adding watermarks, you create a visual signal that your artwork is protected and discourage unauthorized distribution.

Copyright Considerations for Digital Art

Understanding copyright is essential for every artist to ensure they retain ownership of their work and can take legal action if necessary. Copyright grants you the exclusive right to reproduce, distribute, and display your artwork. In the context of digital art, it is important to recognize how copyright works and how to safeguard your rights.

Key Points to Consider Regarding Copyright:

Automatic Copyright:

- In most countries, copyright protection is automatic as soon as you create an original work of art and fix it in a tangible form (i.e., a digital file). You do not need to formally register the work, although registering with a national copyright office can provide additional legal protection.

Licensing Your Artwork:

- When sharing your artwork, you can provide licenses to others, which specify how they can use your work. For instance:

Non-commercial use:

- Allows others to view or display your art but prohibits them from using it for commercial purposes.

Commercial use:

- Grants permission to use your art for profit (e.g., in advertisements, merchandise).

Creative Commons Licenses:

- If you choose to allow others to use your work, Creative Commons licenses provide an easy way to specify the terms of use. For example, you can choose a license that allows others to share your work but requires them to credit you as the creator.

Registering Your Art:

- Although copyright protection is automatic, registering your artwork with the relevant copyright office provides legal documentation of your ownership. It can be helpful in case you need to take legal action for infringement.

Steps to Register Your Artwork with Copyright Authorities:

- **Research the Copyright Office in Your Country**: Look up the copyright registration process for your country (e.g., the U.S. Copyright Office, the UK Intellectual Property Office).
- **Submit an Application**: Fill out the required forms, providing detailed information about the artwork, including a description and a copy of the work.

- **Pay the Registration Fee**: Depending on the jurisdiction, there may be a fee associated with copyright registration.
- **Receive Confirmation**: Once your registration is processed, you will receive confirmation, and your artwork will be officially recorded.

Chapter 11: Backing Up Your Portfolio for Safety

In the digital age, your portfolio is more than just a collection of your artwork; it's your professional identity and potentially the foundation of your career. The importance of keeping it safe cannot be overstated. Whether you are an artist, designer, or creator of any kind, your digital files are precious, and losing them could mean losing years of work.

In this chapter, we will explore how to effectively back up your digital portfolio, ensuring that your creative works are safe, easily accessible, and always recoverable, no matter what happens.

Why You Should Always Have a Backup

Backing up your digital portfolio is crucial for several reasons. While OneDrive provides excellent cloud storage and access to your files across multiple devices, there are still risks involved with any form of digital storage.

Unforeseen Failures:

- Even the most reliable cloud services can experience technical glitches, outages, or data corruption. Backing up your portfolio ensures that you won't lose everything due to something beyond your control.

Accidental Deletion:

- It's easy to accidentally delete files or folders while working, and if you don't have a backup, these errors could lead to permanent loss.

Hardware Failures:

- External devices, such as hard drives or computers, can fail. A backup ensures that your data remains safe even if your hardware breaks down.

Data Theft or Cybersecurity Threats:

- Cyber-attacks, hacking, and malware can compromise your online storage, putting your artwork at risk. Backups offer an extra layer of security.

Peace of Mind:

- Knowing your portfolio is safely backed up gives you the peace of mind to focus on your art, rather than constantly worrying about data loss.

A backup is not just about saving space; it's about ensuring that your creative efforts are safeguarded against any unforeseen circumstances.

Automatic Backup Settings in OneDrive

OneDrive's automatic backup settings can help you ensure that your digital portfolio is continuously backed up without having to manually intervene. These settings will automatically upload your files to the cloud, giving you confidence that your artwork is always safely stored. Here's how you can configure OneDrive's automatic backup for your files:

Open OneDrive Settings:

- Start by clicking the OneDrive icon in the taskbar or system tray of your device.
- In the menu that appears, click on "Settings."

OneDrive Settings from Taskbar

Enable Automatic Backup:

- In the settings window, look for the Backup tab.

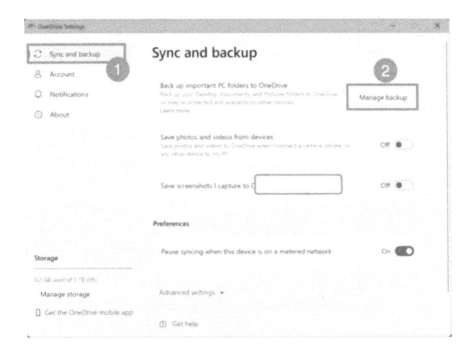

- Under this tab, you will see options to back up your desktop, documents, and pictures.
- Turn on these options to ensure that important folders, such as your portfolio folder, are automatically synced and backed up to OneDrive.

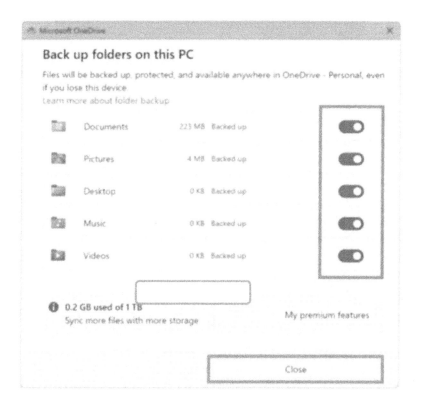

Set Up OneDrive for Folder Synchronization:

- If you use specific folders for organizing your artwork, you can select the folders you want to sync to OneDrive.
- Right-click on a folder, select "Choose OneDrive for Backup," and select the destination folder where you want your artwork saved in the cloud.

Check Sync Status:

- Once enabled, OneDrive will continuously back up your files to the cloud. You can confirm that files are syncing by checking the OneDrive icon for the sync status. A green check mark means the file is fully synced and backed up.

Name	Status
EDITED and PACKAGED by CRISTI.zip	
Excel - Chart Filters.mp4	
Excel - Chart Filters.tscproj	
Excel - Chart Filters.zip	
Filter chart using table in Excel YouTu...	
Filter chart using table in Excel.xlsx	
MVI_0590.MP4	
Rec 02-24-21_001.trec	
Test of Sync.docx	
Thumbnail Chart Filters.xar	
Thumbnail Filter Charts.jpg	

By setting up automatic backups in OneDrive, you ensure that your files are always up-to-date in the cloud without the need for constant monitoring. This way, your portfolio is protected without any extra effort on your part.

Creating Redundant Backups on External Drives or Other Cloud Platforms

While OneDrive is a reliable cloud storage option, diversifying your backup strategy is a smart move. Redundant backups offer an additional layer of security, ensuring that if one backup method fails, you have other options to restore your files. Here's how you can back up your portfolio using external drives and other cloud platforms:

External Drives:
Using an external hard drive or SSD to back up your portfolio is a great way to ensure your files are available offline and protected from cloud-related issues. Here's how to do it:

- Connect your external hard drive to your computer.
- Manually copy your important portfolio folders from your OneDrive folder to the external drive.
- You can also set up an automatic backup using software such as Windows Backup or Time Machine (on Mac) to back up your files to the external drive.

Cloud Redundancy:

- To add another layer of security, you can use a second cloud storage service to back up your portfolio. This could be Google Drive, Dropbox, or another reputable cloud service. By storing your files in multiple cloud platforms, you reduce the risk of losing your data if one service encounters problems.
- Choose a second cloud storage provider and set up a folder specifically for your portfolio.
- Upload your most critical files and artworks to this secondary cloud service, either manually or through syncing software.

Hybrid Backup Strategy:

- Combining both external drives and multiple cloud storage platforms is the best way to ensure redundancy. This method provides the benefits of offline backups and the convenience of cloud access, giving you the ultimate level of protection.

By creating redundant backups, you ensure that your portfolio is protected from multiple angles. You have the security of OneDrive's cloud backup, plus an external drive and a second cloud service. Even if one of these methods fails, you will still have your files safe and accessible.

Restoring Lost or Deleted Files in OneDrive

While having a backup is essential, it's equally important to know how to restore your lost or deleted files in OneDrive. OneDrive has robust tools to help you recover files in case of an accidental deletion or a data loss. Here's how to restore your files:

Restore Deleted Files from the Recycle Bin:

If you accidentally delete a file or folder from OneDrive, it doesn't disappear immediately. Instead, it goes to the Recycle Bin.

- To restore deleted items, go to the OneDrive website and sign in.
- In the left-hand panel, click on the Recycle Bin.
- Browse the deleted items and select the files or folders you want to restore.

- Click Restore to recover the deleted items back to their original location in your OneDrive.

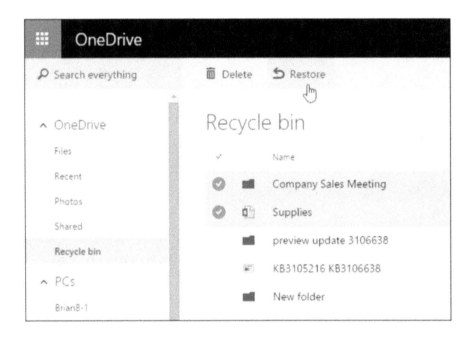

Using OneDrive Version History to Recover Older Versions:

OneDrive also allows you to restore previous versions of a file, which can be helpful if you accidentally overwrite or change something in your artwork.

- To access version history, right-click the file in OneDrive and select Version History.

- You will see a list of all previous versions of the file, complete with timestamps. Select the version you want to restore and click Restore.

Click on the three dots and choose **Restore**.

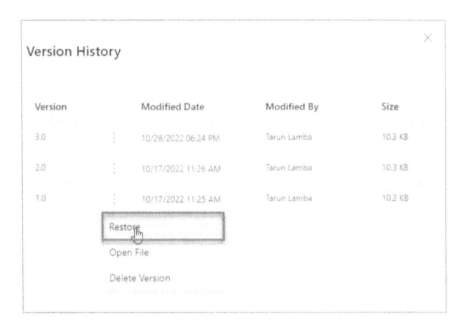

Version History

Version		Modified Date	Modified By	Size
3.0	⋮	10/28/2022 06:24 PM	Tarun Lamba	10.3 KB
2.0	⋮	10/17/2022 11:26 AM	Tarun Lamba	10.3 KB
1.0	⋮	10/17/2022 11:25 AM	Tarun Lamba	10.2 KB

Restore
Open File
Delete Version

Restore from a Previous Backup:

If you have backed up your portfolio on an external drive or another cloud platform, you can restore the files by transferring them back to OneDrive or your device.

- Simply plug in the external drive or sign into the secondary cloud service and retrieve the files.

Having these recovery options ensures that you won't lose your portfolio, even if something goes wrong. By regularly backing up your artwork, both online and offline, and understanding how to recover lost files, you can focus on your creative process without worrying about data loss.

Conclusion

Backing up your portfolio is an essential practice for protecting your artwork and ensuring its availability in the event of unexpected failures or errors. By taking advantage of OneDrive's automatic backup features, using redundant backups with external drives and other cloud platforms, and knowing how to restore lost or deleted files, you ensure that your creative works are always safe, secure, and accessible.

Chapter 12: Keeping Your Portfolio Updated and Relevant

As an artist, your portfolio is more than just a collection of your work; it is a representation of who you are and what you can offer. Just like any professional, your portfolio needs to evolve as you grow in skill, explore new creative directions, or shift your focus within the art world. Regular updates ensure that your portfolio stays relevant, fresh, and reflective of your current abilities and style. In this chapter, we will explore why keeping your portfolio updated is crucial for your success, and we'll discuss strategies to help you manage and refresh your portfolio with ease.

Why Regular Updates Matter for Artists

A static portfolio can quickly become outdated, potentially sending the wrong message to clients, collaborators, or potential buyers. An up-to-date portfolio ensures that you are presenting the most accurate and polished version of your work, which is essential for several reasons:

- **Demonstrates Growth**: Art is an ever-evolving process, and an updated portfolio showcases how your style, technique, and concepts have developed over time. It provides a tangible representation of your progress and professional growth.
- **Attracts New Opportunities**: New works attract new clients, collaborations, and exhibitions. Keeping your portfolio fresh ensures that it reflects your most recent and relevant work, which can open doors to new professional opportunities.
- **Staying Competitive**: The art world is dynamic, and competition can be fierce. Regular updates allow you to stay competitive by continually showcasing your best work, helping you stand out in a crowded market.
- **Avoids Stagnation**: If your portfolio contains outdated or irrelevant work, it could give the impression that you are stagnant or have stopped creating. A regularly updated portfolio indicates that you are an active artist who is constantly exploring new ideas and techniques.
- **Reflects Professionalism**: An updated portfolio is a reflection of your commitment to your art career. It shows potential clients, curators, and employers that you take your practice seriously and are proactive in keeping your presentation sharp and polished.

In summary, regular updates are an essential aspect of maintaining a professional and engaging portfolio. Without them, your portfolio risks becoming a representation of your past rather than a tool for advancing your art career.

Scheduling Portfolio Updates

To ensure that your portfolio stays current, it's important to develop a regular schedule for updating your work. The key to managing this process is consistency and planning. Without a clear strategy, it can be easy to overlook this crucial aspect of your artistic practice. Here are some practical guidelines for scheduling portfolio updates:

Set a Fixed Timeline:

- Schedule regular intervals for reviewing and updating your portfolio. Depending on how frequently you create new work, this could be monthly, quarterly, or bi-annually. For example, if you are consistently producing artwork, aim to refresh your portfolio every three months. This way, your portfolio will always feature recent work without overwhelming you with constant updates.

Review After Major Projects or Exhibitions:

- If you've just completed a large body of work or participated in a significant exhibition, take time to update your portfolio soon after. The new pieces from these projects will likely be some of your strongest, and incorporating them into your portfolio quickly will help you capitalize on the momentum and recognition.

Create a "Portfolio Day" Routine:

- Consider dedicating one day a month or every few months as "Portfolio Day." On this day, review your entire portfolio, make necessary updates, and add any new work. By making it a part of your routine, you will stay on top of it and not let the task slip through the cracks.

Set Reminders:

- Use digital tools such as a calendar or task manager to remind you when it's time to update your portfolio. OneDrive can sync with your calendar, and you can set up automatic reminders to keep track of your portfolio review schedule. These reminders will ensure that you don't forget to make updates as part of your ongoing art practice.

By scheduling your portfolio updates, you can avoid the pressure of last-minute changes and stay on top of maintaining a current, relevant collection of your best work.

Removing Outdated Work While Keeping an Archive

As you create more artwork, some of your older pieces may no longer represent the direction you want to take or might simply not be as strong as your newer work. While it's important to keep your portfolio focused on your best and most current pieces, removing outdated work requires careful consideration. Here are some steps to help you manage the removal of old pieces while preserving their significance in your artistic journey:

Assess the Relevance of Each Piece:

- Take a moment to assess the work in your portfolio. Is it still representative of your current style or skills? Does it align with the message you want your portfolio to convey? If a piece feels out of place or doesn't show your artistic growth, it might be time to remove it.

Remove Without Guilt:

- Removing old work from your portfolio can feel like you're abandoning a part of your artistic history, but it's important to remember that your portfolio is a reflection of where you are now. It's okay to move on from pieces that no longer serve your professional image or goals.

Archive for Personal Reflection or Future Use:

- While removing outdated work from your active portfolio, consider creating a separate archive for pieces that no longer fit but still hold sentimental value or could serve as a future reference. You can store these works on OneDrive, organizing them by date or project so they remain accessible if you ever want to revisit them later.

Maintain an "Archive Folder" in OneDrive:

- OneDrive allows you to organize your art files into folders. Create a dedicated "Archived Portfolio" folder where older work can be stored safely. This keeps your current portfolio clean and focused while preserving the history of your work. When you make updates, move outdated pieces into this folder rather than deleting them entirely.

Evaluate Quality Over Quantity:

- A key element of maintaining a professional portfolio is the quality of the work you showcase. If an older piece no longer aligns with the standard of your current work, remove it to make room for stronger, more relevant pieces. A leaner, more curated portfolio is often more effective than one filled with outdated or less impressive work.

By removing outdated work and archiving it properly, you ensure that your portfolio is always showcasing your most current and high-quality pieces, which will make a stronger impression on potential clients and collaborators.

Tracking Portfolio Engagement and Viewer Statistics

Knowing how your portfolio is being received by visitors can provide valuable insights into what is working and what needs improvement. By tracking engagement and viewer statistics, you can better understand which pieces resonate with your audience and make informed decisions about future updates. Here's how you can track and analyze portfolio engagement:

Use OneDrive's Built-In Analytics (for Share Links):

- When you share a link to your portfolio with clients or prospects, OneDrive allows you to monitor who's viewing your work and when. You can track the number of views, time spent on individual pieces, and which works are being accessed most frequently. This data can help you identify which artwork is generating the most interest and tailor future updates accordingly.

Set Up Google Analytics for Your Portfolio Website:

- If you have a personal website or blog where your portfolio is hosted, setting up Google Analytics can provide detailed insights into how visitors are interacting with your portfolio. You can track page views, bounce rates, and user demographics, all of which help you better understand your audience.

Monitor Social Media Engagement:

- Many artists use social media platforms to promote their portfolios. By tracking likes, comments, shares, and direct messages, you can gauge how well your artwork is performing in the online space. Use this feedback to highlight the works that resonate most with your followers and consider emphasizing these pieces in your main portfolio.

Use Feedback from Clients and Collaborators:

- One of the most insightful ways to gauge engagement is through direct feedback from clients, collaborators, or curators. Pay attention to the comments or critiques you receive, and use them to assess which pieces are most successful and why. If possible, ask for feedback on specific works or sections of your portfolio to gain a clearer understanding of what's working.

Adjust Your Portfolio Based on Engagement:

- Armed with this data, you can make informed decisions about what to showcase in your portfolio. For example, if a particular series of works receives significant engagement, consider making them more prominent in your portfolio. If certain pieces receive little attention, you might want to replace or revise them in future updates.

Tracking portfolio engagement allows you to fine-tune your portfolio to meet the needs of your audience and clients, helping you create a more effective and targeted presentation of your work.

In conclusion, maintaining an up-to-date and relevant portfolio is an essential task for every artist. By scheduling regular updates, removing outdated pieces while archiving them for future reference, and tracking engagement, you ensure that your portfolio remains a powerful tool for showcasing your growth, attracting new opportunities, and staying competitive in the ever-evolving art world. With these strategies, you can keep your portfolio fresh, engaging, and reflective of your artistic journey.

Part 5: Advanced Techniques and Professional Tips

Chapter 13: Using OneDrive with Design & Editing Software

In the creative world, digital artists and designers rely on a variety of software to craft their work. Whether you're a photographer, illustrator, or graphic designer, your workflow typically involves programs like Adobe Photoshop, Illustrator, or Lightroom. Managing these large and complex files can be challenging, but with the right tools, you can streamline your process and keep your work organized, backed up, and easily accessible. OneDrive is an ideal platform for integrating with these design tools, enabling you to save, sync, and manage your files with ease. This chapter will guide you through how to connect OneDrive with your favorite design and editing software, including Photoshop, Illustrator, and Lightroom.

Integrating OneDrive with Photoshop, Illustrator, and Lightroom

OneDrive is not just a cloud storage service but also a powerful tool for enhancing your creative workflow. By integrating OneDrive with popular design and editing software such as Adobe Photoshop,

Illustrator, and Lightroom, you can ensure that your files are always synced, accessible from multiple devices, and securely stored.

Before we go into the specific steps for integration, it's important to understand the role OneDrive can play in your workflow. OneDrive allows you to store your design files in the cloud, which means you can access them from any device with an internet connection. Whether you're working from home, in the office, or on the go, your files are available at your fingertips. Moreover, OneDrive ensures that your work is backed up automatically, so you never have to worry about losing your progress.

Here's a basic overview of how OneDrive integrates with these programs:

Photoshop:

- Photoshop files, especially large PSD files, can quickly become cumbersome, taking up a lot of storage space on your computer. With OneDrive, you can store these files in the cloud, access them on any device, and collaborate with others.

Illustrator:

- Adobe Illustrator's vector files can be large, too, especially when working with intricate designs. Storing these files in OneDrive lets you manage them efficiently and access them from any platform that supports OneDrive.

Lightroom:

- Lightroom is an essential tool for photographers, especially when dealing with large image files. OneDrive helps you store and organize your photos in the cloud, making it easier to access and manage your Lightroom library across multiple devices.

To integrate OneDrive with these design programs, follow these simple steps:

Install OneDrive:

- Ensure that the OneDrive app is installed on your computer. If you're using Windows 10 or 11, OneDrive comes pre-installed. For macOS or older versions of Windows, you can download the OneDrive application from the official website.

Set Up OneDrive Folder:

- Create a dedicated folder within OneDrive for your design files. You might want to organize this folder by project or software, e.g., a "Photoshop" folder, an "Illustrator" folder, and so on.

Sync Design Files:

- Open your design software and start working on your files as usual. When you save your work, navigate to your OneDrive folder and save the files there. This ensures that your files are automatically uploaded to the cloud.

Access Files Across Devices:

- If you need to work on your design files from a different device (e.g., a tablet or laptop), simply log into OneDrive, and all your files will be available.

Saving and Syncing PSD and AI Files in OneDrive

As a designer, you're probably familiar with working with large and complex file types, such as Photoshop's PSD (Photoshop Document) files and Illustrator's AI (Adobe Illustrator) files. These files can be difficult to manage without a proper cloud storage solution. By saving your PSD and AI files in OneDrive, you can benefit from automatic syncing, easy access, and a well-organized portfolio.

Here's how you can save and sync your PSD and AI files in OneDrive:

Organize Your Files:

- First, create a structured folder system in OneDrive. You might want to create separate folders for each project, and within those, separate folders for PSD or AI files. This will help you stay organized and find files quickly when needed.

Save PSD and AI Files to OneDrive:

- When you create or edit a design file in Photoshop or Illustrator, save it directly to your OneDrive folder. In both programs, go to File > Save As and navigate to your OneDrive folder. Once you save the file there, it will automatically upload to the cloud and sync across all your devices.

Ensure Syncing Is Active:

- After saving your files to OneDrive, ensure that your syncing process is active. You can check if your files are syncing by looking at the OneDrive icon in your system tray (on

Windows) or menu bar (on macOS). If the icon shows as "up to date," your files are successfully synced. If there's a syncing issue, you can click on the icon to troubleshoot.

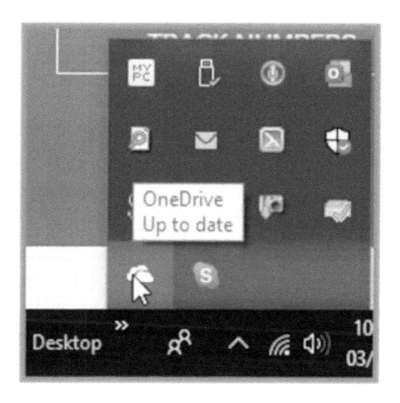

Access Files from Any Device:

- After your files are saved to OneDrive, you can access them from any device, whether it's a desktop computer, tablet, or smartphone. For example, if you want to make a quick tweak to a design while you're away from your computer, simply open OneDrive on your mobile device and make the change. The file will sync automatically, and you can access the latest version when you return to your main workstation.

Backup Your Work:

- Since your files are being saved and synced in OneDrive, they are automatically backed up. OneDrive keeps multiple versions of your files, so if you ever need to revert to a previous version of your work, you can easily do so.

Automating Portfolio Updates with OneDrive and Zapier

As an artist or designer, keeping your portfolio updated can be a time-consuming task. Whether you're working on multiple projects at once or simply need to upload new designs regularly, managing your portfolio's digital presence can be overwhelming. This is where automation tools like Zapier can be incredibly useful.

Zapier is a web-based automation tool that connects different apps and services to automate repetitive tasks. By integrating OneDrive with Zapier, you can automate the process of updating your portfolio without having to do everything manually.

Here's how you can use OneDrive and Zapier to automate your portfolio updates:

- **Sign Up for Zapier:** If you haven't already, create a free account on Zapier. Once you're signed up, you'll be able to create "Zaps" — automated workflows that connect OneDrive with other apps.
- **Create a New Zap:** To start automating your portfolio updates, create a new Zap. A Zap consists of two parts: a trigger and an action. The trigger is an event that will start

the Zap, while the action is the task that will be performed once the trigger occurs.

- **Set OneDrive as the Trigger App**: In this case, the trigger will be something like a new file being uploaded to OneDrive. Select OneDrive as your trigger app, and choose a trigger event such as "New File in Folder" or "New File in Folder (Shared)" depending on your needs.
- **Connect Your OneDrive Account:** Zapier will ask you to sign in to your OneDrive account and allow the app to access your files. Once connected, you can specify which folder within OneDrive will trigger the automation.
- **Choose the Action App**: The action app could be something like a website builder, social media platform, or portfolio platform where you want to display your artwork. For example, you can set up Zapier to automatically upload new files from your OneDrive folder to your personal website or portfolio platform.
- **Set Up the Action:** Specify the action you want to happen once the trigger occurs. For example, if a new design file is uploaded to OneDrive, you can automate the process of adding that file to your portfolio on a website or social media page.
- **Test and Activate the Zap:** Once you've set up your Zap, run a test to make sure everything works as expected. If the test is successful, activate your Zap, and it will run automatically from that point forward.

By using Zapier with OneDrive, you can significantly reduce the time and effort required to update your portfolio, giving you more time to focus on creating new artwork.

Chapter 14: Selling and Licensing Art Using OneDrive

In today's digital age, the way art is sold, licensed, and delivered has evolved significantly. Artists can leverage cloud storage solutions like OneDrive not just for storing their creations, but for securely selling and sharing their artwork with clients, buyers, and collaborators. This chapter will explore how OneDrive can become a key tool for artists in managing sales and licensing agreements, while also facilitating the secure delivery of commissioned artwork.

How to Sell Artwork Using OneDrive as a Storage Hub

OneDrive can be an excellent storage hub when it comes to selling artwork. The first step in this process is using OneDrive to organize and store your artwork in a way that makes it easy to manage, share, and sell. The advantage of OneDrive is its flexibility, security, and ease of use, allowing you to provide a seamless experience for your customers.

Before You Sell:

- **Organize Your Art**: Create a clear folder structure within your OneDrive account. You could categorize your artwork by type (e.g., paintings, digital art, photography) or by collection (e.g., a specific series or project). This structure will help you quickly locate the pieces you want to sell and make them easier to share.
- **Optimize Your Files**: Ensure that your artwork files are properly formatted and of high quality for presentation. Use OneDrive's preview feature to check how your files appear when shared.
- **Consider the File Size**: While OneDrive offers generous storage space, larger files (e.g., high-resolution images) may take longer to upload or may need to be compressed for easier sharing. Make sure your files are easy to access and download by your buyers.

Steps for Selling Artwork Using OneDrive:

- **Upload Your Artwork**: Once your artwork is ready and organized, upload the files to your OneDrive account.
  - To upload, simply drag and drop your artwork files into the OneDrive folder of your choice or use the "Upload" button to select files from your computer.
- **Create a Shareable Link**: Once your artwork is uploaded, generate a shareable link for potential buyers.
  - Right-click the file or folder you want to share and select "Share".

- Choose the appropriate permission settings (whether the buyer can only view or also edit, though for art sales, typically view-only is recommended).
- **Set Permissions**: When generating the shareable link, make sure to set it so that only the intended buyer can access the file.
  - Set permissions to "Anyone with the link" for public access or "Specific people" for exclusive buyers.
- **Send the Link to the Buyer**: Share the generated link with the buyer via email, message, or your preferred communication method. You can even send the link within an invoice or as part of a confirmation email.
- **Invoice and Payment**: Alongside the link, provide your buyer with an invoice that includes payment instructions. Once payment is received, the buyer can access the artwork through the shared OneDrive link.

OneDrive's ability to easily share large files makes it an ideal platform for artists to sell their work, without having to worry about the complications of email attachments or file-size limitations that other platforms may impose.

Sharing Licensing Agreements Through OneDrive

Licensing agreements are essential for artists when it comes to protecting their intellectual property. OneDrive can be used as a platform to securely share licensing contracts with clients, ensuring that both parties are on the same page with terms and conditions.

A **licensing agreement** outlines how the buyer can use the artwork, and it can range from exclusive rights to limited or non-exclusive usage. By using OneDrive, artists can create, share, and store their licensing contracts digitally, maintaining a clear record of agreements for both legal protection and business management.

Before You Share Licensing Agreements:

- **Prepare Your Agreement**: Write a clear and thorough licensing agreement that specifies the terms of usage. This document should include details like the scope of the license, payment terms, duration of use, and any other restrictions on the buyer's use of the artwork.
- **Format for Clarity**: Ensure the agreement is easy to read and understand. Using a professional template or working with a legal advisor to draft the agreement is highly recommended to avoid ambiguity.
- **Store Contracts in OneDrive**: Once the agreement is finalized, upload it to OneDrive to keep it secure and accessible for future reference.

Steps for Sharing Licensing Agreements via OneDrive:

- **Upload the Licensing Agreement to OneDrive**: Store your licensing agreements in a specific folder within OneDrive for easy access and organization. Make sure the file is named appropriately, such as "Licensing Agreement - [Artwork Title]".
- **Share the Agreement with the Client**: Generate a shareable link for the licensing agreement document and send it to your client or buyer.

- o Use the same process as with your artwork—right-click the file, select "Share", and either provide access to specific individuals or allow access to anyone with the link, depending on the agreement type.
- **Set Permissions**: When sharing, ensure that your permissions are set to "View only" so that clients can review the agreement but cannot modify it.
- **Allow the Client to Sign the Agreement**: If your client needs to sign the licensing agreement, you can either use digital signature tools or have them print, sign, and send it back. Alternatively, clients can be instructed to return the signed agreement as a scanned PDF, which can also be uploaded and stored in OneDrive for record-keeping.
- **Keep a Record**: Once the agreement is signed, you can securely store the final document in OneDrive, creating a backup of the original contract for your records. This also ensures that both you and your client have access to a copy of the signed agreement at any time.

By using OneDrive to store and share licensing agreements, artists can streamline their licensing process and maintain organized, easily accessible records of transactions.

Using OneDrive to Deliver Commissioned Artwork Securely

When working with commissioned projects, delivering the final artwork securely is essential. Whether you're completing a custom painting or a digital design, OneDrive offers a safe, reliable way to send completed artwork to clients without the risk of loss or unauthorized access.

With OneDrive, artists can send large files, track access, and maintain control over how their artwork is delivered and used. Clients also benefit from the ability to access their commissioned artwork easily and on their preferred devices.

Before Delivering Commissioned Artwork:

- **Organize Your Files**: Once the commissioned artwork is completed, organize it neatly within your OneDrive folder. You may want to create a separate folder for each commission project to keep things clear.
- **File Format Considerations**: Ensure that the artwork is in a format that suits the client's needs. For digital art, this may be a high-resolution PNG or JPG file. For physical artwork, you might want to provide a scanned or photographed copy.
- **Prepare the Final Files for Delivery**: Before sharing, double-check that the artwork meets the agreed-upon specifications and quality standards.

Steps for Delivering Commissioned Artwork Securely via OneDrive:

- **Upload the Completed Artwork to OneDrive**: Upload the final artwork to your OneDrive account, ensuring it is saved in an organized folder specific to the commission.
- **Generate a Shareable Link**: Create a secure link to the artwork by selecting the file and choosing the "Share"

option. You can share the link with your client via email or a secure messaging platform.

- **Set Viewing Permissions**: Restrict access by setting the permissions so that the client can view but not download or alter the artwork unless you wish to allow them to do so.
- **Notify the Client**: Inform your client via email that their commissioned artwork is ready for delivery and provide them with the link to access the file. You can also include any additional instructions for use or printing if necessary.
- **Confirm the Delivery**: Ask the client to confirm that they've received the artwork and that it meets their expectations. You can set up notifications in OneDrive to be alerted when the file has been accessed.

OneDrive's cloud-based system allows for easy, trackable, and secure delivery of artwork. As long as you maintain control over the shared link, you can be confident that your work is delivered safely and professionally.

Summary

OneDrive provides artists with a powerful tool for securely selling, sharing, and delivering their artwork, while also streamlining the licensing process. By taking advantage of OneDrive's features—like file organization, permission settings, and secure link sharing—artists can manage their business more effectively, ensuring that their artwork and agreements are handled professionally and efficiently. Whether you are selling individual pieces, managing licensing contracts, or delivering commissioned projects, OneDrive makes it easier to stay organized and maintain control over your digital art business.

Chapter 15: Showcasing Art at Online and Physical Exhibitions

In this chapter, we will explore how you can effectively use OneDrive to display and submit your artwork for online and physical exhibitions. We'll go over the processes involved in using OneDrive for organizing your art portfolio, collaborating with curators, and setting up digital displays for in-person art events. These strategies will ensure your artwork is presented in a professional and engaging way, regardless of the exhibition format. Whether your art is being showcased digitally or in a physical space, OneDrive can simplify many of the logistical tasks involved, providing you with the tools to make the most of your exhibitions.

Using OneDrive to Organize and Submit Art for Online Shows

OneDrive provides a powerful platform for storing and sharing your artwork for online exhibitions. Many art shows now accept digital submissions, making it essential to have a well-organized digital portfolio that is easy to submit. With OneDrive, you can not only store your artwork but also prepare it in a way that meets the specific requirements of online exhibition platforms.

Why Organizing Your Artwork Is Crucial

Before submitting artwork to an online exhibition, it is important to have a structured and clearly organized portfolio. Online exhibitions often have strict guidelines for submitting art, such as file type, size, and resolution. OneDrive makes it easy to organize your work in a way that adheres to these requirements.

Here's how you can organize and prepare your artwork for submission:

- **Step 1: Create a Dedicated Folder**
  Start by creating a separate folder within OneDrive specifically for your exhibition submissions. This helps keep your work organized and ensures you don't mix up your personal projects with exhibition materials.
- To create a folder, open OneDrive and select the option to create a new folder.
- Name the folder something specific to the exhibition, such as "2025 Online Art Show Submission."

Step 2: Prepare Your Artwork

- Ensure each piece of artwork is in the correct file format (usually JPEG, PNG, or TIFF for images). You may need to resize or adjust the resolution of your files to meet the exhibition's criteria.

- For most online shows, images should be high-resolution (usually 300 dpi) to maintain quality when viewed at different sizes.
- If necessary, use image editing software to adjust colors or improve the quality of your artwork.

Step 3: Add Metadata

- Adding metadata, such as a title, description, and tags to each image, will help the exhibition organizers understand your artwork better. This is particularly useful when the curators or reviewers are browsing through multiple submissions.
- Right-click on each file in OneDrive and choose the "Properties" or "Details" option to add information like the title of the artwork, the medium used, and any relevant keywords.

Step 4: Generate a Shareable Link

- After preparing your files, you can easily generate a shareable link for each piece of artwork or for the entire folder. This link is what you will submit to the exhibition organizers.
- Right-click on your folder or specific files, and select the "Share" option.
- Choose the appropriate sharing settings, ensuring you have enabled view-only access, which allows curators to see your work without making any changes to your files.

Step 5: Submit the Link to the Exhibition

- Once you have your links ready, follow the online exhibition's submission guidelines to submit your artwork. Many platforms accept a URL or a shared folder link, so pasting your OneDrive link into the submission form will usually suffice.

By following these steps, you ensure that your digital submission is professional, well-organized, and easy for exhibition organizers to view.

Collaborating with Curators via OneDrive

OneDrive is an excellent tool for collaborating with curators when preparing for an online or physical art exhibition. Whether you're fine-tuning a selection of works or seeking feedback, OneDrive allows for seamless collaboration with others involved in the exhibition process.

How OneDrive Facilitates Collaboration

When collaborating with curators, clear communication and easy access to your work are key. OneDrive allows for real-time updates, comments, and file sharing, which simplifies the process of receiving feedback and making revisions to your work.

Here's how to effectively collaborate with curators via OneDrive:

Step 1: Share a Folder for Collaboration

- The first step is to create a shared folder in OneDrive where both you and the curator can upload and view artwork.

This eliminates the need for email attachments or multiple file versions.

- Create a folder specifically for the exhibition and share it with the curator by clicking the "Share" option.
- Choose the setting that allows the curator to either view or edit the files, depending on your needs.

Step 2: Add Comments and Feedback

- One of the benefits of using OneDrive is the ability to leave comments on specific files. As a curator reviews your artwork, they can add notes directly to the image, making it easy for you to address their feedback.
- To add a comment, open the file and click on the "Comments" section.
- Type your feedback or reply directly to the curator's comments.

Step 3: Work on Revisions Together

- Once the curator has given feedback, you can make revisions directly to the file. Since OneDrive syncs automatically across devices, both you and the curator will be able to see updated versions of your work in real-time.
- Upload new versions of your artwork as needed and delete older versions to keep the folder clean and organized.
- If a file needs to be adjusted, edit it on your device and the changes will be automatically reflected in the shared folder.

Step 4: Track Revisions

- OneDrive keeps track of previous versions of files, so if you need to revert to an earlier version of a piece, it's easy to do so.
- Right-click on any file in OneDrive and select "Version History."
- This feature allows you to go back to previous versions of the artwork if necessary, helping you track changes over time.
- By using these features, you can maintain an organized, transparent, and efficient collaboration process with curators, ensuring your artwork meets the exhibition's requirements while benefiting from expert feedback.

Setting Up Digital Displays for Physical Art Exhibitions

OneDrive doesn't just help with online exhibitions; it can also play a key role in setting up digital displays for physical art shows. Many galleries and exhibition spaces now feature digital displays or projectors that allow artists to showcase their work in a dynamic, interactive way. Using OneDrive to set up these digital displays ensures your art is presented professionally and easily accessible to the audience.

Steps to Setting Up Digital Displays

Whether you're setting up a slideshow on a digital screen or projecting your artwork onto a wall, OneDrive allows you to store, organize, and display your art efficiently. Here's how to use OneDrive for this purpose:

Step 1: Organize Artwork for Display

- Before the exhibition, organize the digital versions of your artwork into a folder in OneDrive. If the exhibition requires a specific order, such as by theme or chronology, make sure to arrange the files accordingly.
- Create a folder for each series or group of works and name the files in a clear sequence (e.g., "Painting 1," "Painting 2," etc.).

Step 2: Choose the Right File Format

- Depending on the display setup, you may need to convert your artwork into a video, slideshow, or interactive gallery. OneDrive supports various file formats such as images, videos, and presentations. You can create a slideshow using PowerPoint or a video using editing software and upload it to OneDrive for easy access.
- If using PowerPoint, save your presentation in the correct format (e.g., .pptx or .mp4) and upload it to your OneDrive folder.
- If the exhibition uses a projector, ensure that your files are high-quality and formatted for large-scale display.

Step 3: Share the Folder with Event Coordinators

- Once your artwork is uploaded and organized, you can share the folder with the event coordinators or gallery staff who are responsible for setting up the display. This ensures they have access to the correct files and can download them directly from OneDrive.

- Share the folder by clicking on the "Share" button and generating a link that can be sent to the exhibition organizers.

Step 4: Ensure Smooth Playback During the Exhibition

- On the day of the exhibition, make sure the digital display equipment is set up and tested in advance. Ensure that your art is displayed correctly, and there are no file compatibility issues.
- Test your slideshow or video presentation using the gallery's digital equipment before the event opens to the public.
- Keep a backup copy of your files on a USB drive or external hard drive, just in case you encounter technical issues with the digital display.
- Using OneDrive for setting up digital displays ensures that your artwork is shown seamlessly, maintaining its integrity while allowing for easy adjustments and updates as needed.

By utilizing OneDrive in these ways, you streamline the process of showcasing your art both online and in physical spaces. Whether submitting to online exhibitions, collaborating with curators, or setting up digital displays at a gallery, OneDrive's cloud storage and sharing capabilities provide all the tools needed to ensure your artwork is presented professionally.

Appendices & Glossary

Appendix A: OneDrive Keyboard Shortcuts

In today's fast-paced digital environment, efficiency is key—especially for artists who need to manage and organize their artwork seamlessly. OneDrive provides a variety of keyboard shortcuts designed to make navigation faster and more intuitive. By using these shortcuts, you can streamline your workflow, save time, and avoid unnecessary clicks. Whether you are uploading new artwork, organizing your portfolio, or sharing files, these shortcuts will help you achieve tasks quickly and with minimal effort.

Understanding keyboard shortcuts is like learning a new language for your software. Once you familiarize yourself with these commands, your interaction with OneDrive will be smoother and more efficient. In this section, we will explore a selection of the most useful OneDrive keyboard shortcuts, categorize them by their functionality, and guide you through how each can help optimize your work process.

1. Useful Shortcuts for Faster Navigation

OneDrive's navigation shortcuts are designed to help you move through the application's interface quickly. Instead of relying solely on your mouse or touchpad, these shortcuts allow you to jump to different sections and perform tasks with just a few key presses. By incorporating these shortcuts into your daily routine, you can move between folders, search your files, and interact with the user interface much faster.

Navigating Between Folders

Alt + Left Arrow
This shortcut lets you quickly go back to the previous folder you were viewing. It's particularly helpful when you need to retrace your steps while organizing or reviewing artwork in different directories.

Alt + Right Arrow
In contrast to the back navigation, this shortcut lets you move forward to the next folder if you've previously used the back command.

Tab (Next Element) + Shift + Tab (Previous Element)
These commands allow you to jump between clickable elements within the OneDrive window. Pressing Tab will move to the next item, such as a button, a link, or a text field, while Shift + Tab will take you to the previous element. This is ideal for navigating forms or interacting with various options without needing to use a mouse.

Accessing File and Folder Options

Enter
Pressing Enter while highlighting a file or folder will open it or activate it. If you are in a folder, this shortcut will bring you inside that folder to view its contents. It's a quick way to enter a

directory without needing to double-click on the folder with your mouse.

Shift + F10
This shortcut opens the context menu for the selected file or folder. It's equivalent to right-clicking on a file or folder with the mouse. From this menu, you can access options such as renaming, deleting, moving, or sharing the file.

Ctrl + C (Copy), Ctrl + X (Cut), Ctrl + V (Paste)
These are standard shortcuts for copying, cutting, and pasting items. They work across OneDrive, allowing you to quickly copy or move files and folders from one location to another. This is useful when you need to duplicate files, or reorganize your portfolio quickly.

Searching and Filtering Files

Ctrl + E
This shortcut places the cursor in the search bar at the top of the OneDrive interface, allowing you to start typing immediately to search for files or folders. If you're looking for a specific piece of artwork or project, this shortcut will help you find it much faster.

Ctrl + F
While using OneDrive, you can press Ctrl + F to open the search box for finding content on the current page. This is especially useful when you are browsing through a large folder or document and need to locate a particular file.

Managing Files and Folders

Ctrl + A
Pressing Ctrl + A will select all the items in your current folder or directory. This is especially helpful when you want to move, copy, or delete all items in a folder, such as when cleaning up or organizing your portfolio.

Delete
When a file or folder is selected, pressing the Delete key will send it to the Recycle Bin. This shortcut saves time compared to right-clicking and selecting the delete option from the context menu.

Ctrl + Z (Undo), Ctrl + Y (Redo)
These classic shortcuts work in OneDrive just as they do in most other applications. If you make an error while editing, uploading, or organizing your artwork, pressing Ctrl + Z will undo the last action. If you undo something by mistake, Ctrl + Y allows you to redo that action. This is vital for protecting your work from accidental changes.

2. Speeding Up File Sharing and Collaboration

When collaborating with others or sharing your artwork, time is of the essence. OneDrive offers shortcuts that make sharing and working together more efficient.

Ctrl + Shift + S
This shortcut opens the "Share" dialog box for the selected file or folder, allowing you to quickly send your work to clients, collaborators, or friends. Once the dialog box is open, you can choose permissions, add email addresses, and send the link right away.

Ctrl + Shift + N

Use this shortcut to create a new folder directly within OneDrive. By organizing your artwork into multiple folders for different themes, projects, or clients, you can easily manage your portfolio and keep it neatly arranged.

3. Miscellaneous Shortcuts

Ctrl + P (Print)

If you need to print a document or image stored in your OneDrive account, press Ctrl + P. This will open the print dialog, allowing you to select your printer and adjust print settings before printing.

Alt + D

Pressing Alt + D will highlight the address bar at the top of the OneDrive page. This shortcut can be useful when you want to copy the URL of your current folder or file for sharing or reference.

F5 (Refresh)

Pressing F5 refreshes the OneDrive page, ensuring that you're seeing the most up-to-date information, especially after uploading new files, changing permissions, or editing documents. This keeps your workflow up-to-date without needing to manually reload the page.

4. General Navigation and Viewing

Ctrl + + (Zoom In), Ctrl + - (Zoom Out)

These shortcuts are useful when you want to adjust the zoom level of your OneDrive interface. Whether you're on a small laptop screen or a large desktop monitor, these shortcuts let you enlarge or shrink the interface to suit your needs.

F11 (Full-Screen Mode)

Pressing F11 will toggle OneDrive into full-screen mode. This is particularly helpful when you want to focus on viewing your artwork or portfolio without distractions from the browser's address bar or toolbar.

Appendix B: Troubleshooting Common OneDrive Issues

In this section, we will discuss some common issues that users face when using OneDrive, and we will provide simple and clear solutions for each. OneDrive is a powerful tool for managing and sharing digital portfolios, but occasionally, issues can arise that can interrupt your workflow. Understanding how to address these issues will ensure that you can keep your digital art portfolio well-managed, secure, and accessible at all times.

File Not Uploading? Here's What to Do

It's not uncommon to encounter problems when uploading files to OneDrive. Whether it's due to file size, internet connectivity, or other issues, it's essential to identify the cause and take appropriate action to resolve it.

Possible Causes and Solutions

- **Check Your Internet Connection**:
  A weak or interrupted internet connection can prevent

your files from uploading. If you are experiencing slow uploads, check your internet connection to ensure it's stable. You can restart your modem or router to improve connectivity.

- o **Solution**: Try uploading a small file first to confirm that your connection is stable. If the upload works, the issue may have been a temporary connection issue.

- **File Size is Too Large**:
OneDrive has limits on file sizes, depending on the subscription plan. If your file exceeds the upload limit, it will not upload to OneDrive.
  - o **Solution**: Check the file size and compare it with OneDrive's maximum upload limit. For free users, the upload limit is typically 100 GB per file, while for paid plans, it can be higher. If the file is too large, consider compressing it or splitting it into smaller parts using software like WinRAR or 7zip.

- **File Name Issues**:
Sometimes the issue might be with the file name. OneDrive has restrictions on special characters in file names, which can cause an upload to fail.
  - o **Solution**: Ensure that your file names do not include special characters such as slashes (/), question marks (?), or asterisks (*). Renaming the file to remove any problematic characters should resolve the issue.

- **Storage Space**:
If your OneDrive storage is full, you won't be able to upload any new files.

- Solution: Check your available storage in the OneDrive settings. If your storage is full, you can delete unnecessary files, empty your Recycle Bin, or upgrade to a larger storage plan.

Syncing Issues and How to Fix Them

Syncing issues are one of the most common problems that OneDrive users encounter. Syncing ensures that all your files are up to date across all devices, so if syncing fails, it can cause discrepancies in your art portfolio.

Common Syncing Problems and Solutions

- **Files Aren't Syncing Across Devices**:
  If your files are not syncing between devices, the issue could be due to a variety of factors such as incorrect settings or connection issues.
  - **Solution**: Ensure that OneDrive is properly set up and running on all devices. You should verify that you are logged into the same OneDrive account across all your devices. Additionally, check if the syncing process is paused or if there are any updates pending.
  - **To check syncing status**: Open the OneDrive app or desktop client and look for the sync icon. If it's paused, click on the icon and choose the option to resume syncing.

- **OneDrive Showing Sync Errors**:
  OneDrive may display an error icon next to a file or folder if it's having trouble syncing.
  - o **Solution**: If you see a sync error message, right-click the OneDrive icon in your system tray (for Windows) or menu bar (for Mac), and select **View Sync Problems**. OneDrive will show you the files with issues and give you specific suggestions on how to fix them. You may need to move, rename, or delete the problematic files, or check your internet connection.
- **Conflicting Versions of Files**:
  Sometimes, when a file is edited on multiple devices, OneDrive can create duplicate or conflicting versions of the same file.
  - o **Solution**: If OneDrive detects a conflict, it will save both versions of the file. You can review the conflicting files and choose the correct version. OneDrive allows you to merge changes or manually delete one of the versions.
- **Unresponsive OneDrive App**:
  If the OneDrive app is not syncing or responding, it could be because of outdated software or other software conflicts.
  - o **Solution**: Make sure that both the OneDrive app and your operating system are up to date. If the problem persists, try reinstalling the OneDrive app. Uninstalling and reinstalling OneDrive can often resolve issues caused by corrupted files or settings.

Recovering Lost or Deleted Files

One of the main advantages of using cloud storage like OneDrive is the ability to recover lost or deleted files. However, understanding how to retrieve them and how long they are recoverable is essential to ensure that your art portfolio stays intact.

How to Recover Deleted Files

Check the Recycle Bin:

- When you delete a file on OneDrive, it is typically sent to the Recycle Bin. If you realize that you have accidentally deleted a file, it's easy to restore it.

Solution:

- Go to the **OneDrive website** and navigate to the **Recycle Bin**.
- Select the files you wish to restore.
- Click **Restore** to bring the files back to their original location.

File Recovery After a Longer Period:

- If the files were deleted from the Recycle Bin more than 30 days ago, they may not appear in the Recycle Bin. However, OneDrive offers an option to recover files using the **OneDrive Rewind** feature.

Solution:

OneDrive Rewind: This feature allows you to restore your entire OneDrive to a previous version, which can be useful if you've lost a significant amount of work. To use Rewind:

- Open the OneDrive app or website.
- Select **Settings**, then **Restore your OneDrive**.
- Choose a date when your files were intact, and OneDrive will restore everything to that point.

Using Version History to Recover Older Versions of a File:

- If a file has been edited, and you want to recover an earlier version, OneDrive allows you to revert to a previous version. This is particularly useful if you made changes to a piece of artwork that you want to undo.

Solution:

- Right-click the file in OneDrive and select **Version History**.
- Browse through the available versions and choose the one you wish to restore.
- Click **Restore** to revert to that version.

Contacting OneDrive Support:

- If you cannot find a deleted file in the Recycle Bin and you cannot restore it using Rewind, you may need to contact OneDrive support for additional help. They may be able to assist you in retrieving the file from their backup systems.

Appendix C: Additional Resources for Artists

This section is designed to guide you through a collection of invaluable resources that can help enhance your digital portfolio, inspire your artistic endeavors, and expand your reach within the art world. Below are some recommendations that will assist you in growing and sharing your art with a wider audience, from finding inspiration for your portfolio to selling your work online and utilizing software tools for maximum productivity and presentation.

Recommended Websites for Portfolio Inspiration

As an artist, one of the most important aspects of creating a digital portfolio is ensuring it stands out and accurately represents your style and skill. Sometimes, inspiration can come from other artists and their presentations. The following websites provide excellent examples of creative portfolios and offer a wealth of ideas on how to structure and showcase your own work.

Behance

Behance is one of the most popular platforms for showcasing creative portfolios. It allows artists from all disciplines—whether visual art, graphic design, photography, or even architecture—to upload their work and get noticed. Browsing other portfolios on Behance can offer you fresh ideas for layout, organization, and even how to display your creative process.

Why use it?

Behance also features a large community where you can interact with other professionals, get feedback, and connect with potential clients.

Dribbble

If you're a designer or illustrator, Dribbble is a fantastic platform for showing off your best work. The website has a strong focus on visual design and allows artists to post small "shots" of their projects. This format makes it easier for people to quickly view and appreciate the essence of your work.

Why use it?

Dribbble's interactive community is a great space to share work, receive constructive feedback, and even get hired for freelance projects.

Adobe Portfolio

Adobe Portfolio is a service included with Adobe Creative Cloud, enabling you to build a fully customizable portfolio without needing any coding experience. It has a variety of templates designed to showcase artwork, photography, or design projects beautifully.

Why use it?
You can easily integrate it with other Adobe apps, like Lightroom and Photoshop, making it ideal for photographers and graphic designers who rely heavily on Adobe products.

ArtStation
For digital artists, concept artists, and illustrators, ArtStation is a powerful platform that showcases highly polished portfolios. It is widely recognized in the industry, particularly in the realms of game design, animation, and visual effects.

Why use it?
ArtStation's marketplace also allows you to sell digital artwork or offer services to clients, making it a perfect platform for professional digital artists.

Cargo
Cargo offers an easy-to-use website builder, providing flexible and visually appealing templates for creating a personalized portfolio. It is great for fine artists, graphic designers, and even those in the fashion industry who need a clean, professional platform to show their work.

Why use it?
Cargo offers customizable themes and layouts that can be tailored to your needs, giving you full control over the appearance of your portfolio.

By exploring these platforms, you can find ways to improve the presentation of your work and learn from other successful artists in the field. These websites will not only inspire you but also provide a space for you to interact with like-minded individuals and engage with a larger creative community.

Best Online Marketplaces to Sell Art

Once you've created a stunning digital portfolio and refined your artwork, the next step is to get your art in front of potential buyers. Fortunately, there are numerous online platforms where artists can showcase and sell their creations, from digital prints to original pieces. Here are some of the best online marketplaces to consider for selling your art.

Etsy

Etsy is one of the largest and most well-known online marketplaces for handmade goods, vintage items, and art. The platform allows artists to set up a shop, upload their work, and sell directly to buyers.

Why use it?

Etsy's vast audience provides a great opportunity for artists to sell to people looking for unique, handcrafted, or one-of-a-kind pieces. Additionally, Etsy offers strong search optimization tools to help customers find your products.

Saatchi Art

If you're looking to sell fine art, Saatchi Art is a global marketplace with a focus on high-quality, original pieces. Artists can upload their work and set their prices, while buyers are encouraged to purchase original artworks or prints.

Why use it?

Saatchi Art has a large, global customer base that includes collectors, interior designers, and art enthusiasts. The platform also offers a print-on-demand service, enabling you to sell reproductions of your art without having to handle printing or shipping yourself.

Redbubble

Redbubble is ideal for artists who want to sell their designs on a variety of products, including t-shirts, mugs, phone cases, and more. It's a great option if you're interested in diversifying your revenue streams by offering your art in a range of formats.

Why use it?

Redbubble handles all the printing and shipping, so you can focus on creating designs and promoting your work. It's particularly suitable for illustrators, graphic designers, and digital artists.

Artfinder

Artfinder is another excellent marketplace for original artwork, with a focus on handmade, one-of-a-kind pieces. It's a curated platform, which means your work must go through an approval process before being listed for sale.

Why use it?

The platform emphasizes high-quality, authentic art, so it's perfect if you're looking to sell original paintings, sculptures, or mixed media art. It also helps you reach a more targeted audience of serious art buyers.

Fine Art America

This site allows you to sell original works of art, prints, and even home decor featuring your designs. Fine Art America also lets you set up your own personal online store to showcase and sell your work.

Why use it?

It offers extensive options for artists, including print-on-demand services, marketing tools, and global shipping, which makes it easy to manage your art sales.

Zazzle

Similar to Redbubble, Zazzle allows artists to create and sell custom designs on a wide array of products. If you're looking to reach a broader audience with your work, Zazzle provides an easy-to-use platform for artists to showcase their designs on everything from apparel to stationery.

Why use it?

Zazzle's expansive marketplace and diverse product range can help you reach different types of customers. It also has a robust customization system, allowing customers to personalize your designs.

By using these online marketplaces, you can begin selling your artwork and earning income. Consider choosing platforms that best match your art style, whether you specialize in fine art, graphic design, or digital prints.

Software & Tools to Enhance Digital Portfolios

Creating a professional digital portfolio requires more than just uploading artwork. To truly showcase your art in the best light, you'll need powerful software and tools to enhance, organize, and present your work. The following are essential tools that will help take your digital portfolio to the next level.

Adobe Photoshop

Adobe Photoshop is one of the most popular image-editing tools for artists. It offers powerful features that allow you to edit, enhance, and manipulate your artwork in endless ways. Whether you are a photographer, painter, or graphic designer, Photoshop has the tools needed to polish and refine your art.

Why use it?

With its vast array of brushes, filters, and editing options, Photoshop is perfect for creating and optimizing high-quality images for your portfolio.

Adobe Lightroom

For photographers, Adobe Lightroom is a must-have tool. It's designed specifically for editing and organizing photos in a way that allows you to maintain the highest image quality.

Why use it?

Lightroom offers non-destructive editing, so you can adjust your photos without permanently altering the original file. It also includes a robust system for cataloging your work, which is ideal when managing large collections of artwork.

Canva

Canva is an easy-to-use graphic design tool that allows you to create stunning visuals, presentations, and portfolio templates. While not as advanced as Photoshop, Canva is perfect for creating sleek, professional-looking layouts for digital portfolios.

Why use it?

It's great for beginners or anyone who wants to create eye-catching designs quickly. You can also use Canva to design business cards, social media graphics, and promotional materials.

Procreate

For digital illustrators and painters, Procreate is a powerful and user-friendly drawing app. Available on the iPad, Procreate offers intuitive drawing tools, brushes, and a variety of features to help you create beautiful digital art.

Why use it?

Procreate is perfect for creating original artwork that you can easily upload to your portfolio. It's portable, allowing you to work on your art wherever you go.

Trello

When managing a digital portfolio with multiple pieces and projects, Trello can be a great way to stay organized. This project management tool lets you set up boards, lists, and cards to track your progress, deadlines, and to-do lists.

Why use it?

Trello is an excellent tool for managing your portfolio development process, ensuring that all tasks are completed on time and nothing is overlooked.

Google Drive

Google Drive offers cloud storage and collaboration tools that can be beneficial when managing large files or sharing your portfolio with others. You can store your artwork, share it with clients, and collaborate with other artists or professionals.

Why use it?

It's perfect for artists who need secure cloud storage with easy sharing options. Plus, with Google Docs and Sheets, you can track project details and timelines.

These resources, tools, and platforms are all designed to help you build a digital portfolio that not only showcases your work beautifully but also supports the process of sharing, selling, and expanding your artistic reach. By utilizing the suggestions outlined in this section, you'll be better prepared to present your art to the world and manage your professional art career with efficiency and ease.

Appendix D: OneDrive Storage Plans & Pricing Comparison

In this section, we will explore the different OneDrive storage plans available and compare them to help you determine which option is best suited for your needs as an artist. Whether you're storing a small collection of digital artwork or managing a large portfolio with high-resolution images and videos, understanding your storage options is crucial for making the right decision.

OneDrive offers various plans designed to cater to different users, including both free and paid options. Each plan comes with a unique set of features, including storage capacity, file-sharing options, and access to additional tools and services. Understanding the differences between these plans can help you choose the one that aligns best with your specific needs.

Free vs. Paid Plans

1. Free Plan:

The free OneDrive plan is a great starting point for individuals who need basic cloud storage capabilities. While it offers limited storage, it's sufficient for users with smaller portfolios or those just getting started with digital art storage and sharing.

Storage Space:

- The free OneDrive plan provides you with **5 GB of storage**. This may be enough for a few high-resolution images or some basic artwork, but it will likely fill up quickly if you have a growing portfolio or large files such as videos or high-definition images.

File Sharing:

- You can easily upload files, organize them in folders, and share them with others. However, file-sharing capabilities are somewhat limited compared to paid plans, and there are restrictions on how many people you can share files with at once.

Access to Office Online Apps:

- The free plan also gives you access to Microsoft Office Online apps like Word, Excel, and PowerPoint, which can be useful if you need to create simple documents or presentations for your artwork. However, these tools are limited in functionality compared to the desktop versions available in paid plans.

Limitations:

- Since you're limited to only 5 GB of storage, you may find yourself needing to upgrade as your portfolio grows, especially if you plan to store high-quality images, videos, or other media files. The free plan also lacks some of the advanced features found in the paid plans, such as advanced file versioning and additional collaboration tools.

---

2. Paid Plans:

OneDrive's paid plans offer increased storage capacity, advanced sharing options, and additional features that can be extremely beneficial for artists. These plans come in various tiers, each designed for different needs and budgets. Let's take a closer look at the key features of each paid plan:

Personal Plans:

OneDrive Standalone 100 GB Plan:

This plan offers **100 GB of storage**, providing significantly more space than the free plan. It's ideal for individuals who need extra room but don't require the full range of features offered in the higher-tier plans.

- **Storage Space:** 100 GB is ideal for small to medium portfolios, including images, documents, and videos. While it won't be sufficient for large-scale art portfolios with many files, it's a good choice for an artist who's starting to move more of their work to the cloud and wants more room for storage.

- **Cost:** This plan is typically more affordable than the more extensive options, offering a good balance between cost and storage capacity.
- **File Sharing:** This plan includes more robust sharing options than the free plan. You can share files and folders with multiple people, and you get more control over permissions and access levels.

Microsoft 365 Personal:

If you need additional features, the **Microsoft 365 Personal plan** provides 1 TB of storage, plus access to the full suite of Microsoft Office apps (Word, Excel, PowerPoint, and Outlook). This is ideal for artists who need to do more than just store their art; they may also want to create presentations or business documents.

- **Storage Space:** With 1 TB of storage, you have ample room for thousands of high-resolution images, videos, and documents. This is perfect for larger portfolios or artists who regularly produce high-quality files that need ample storage space.
- **Cost:** The Microsoft 365 Personal plan comes with a higher price tag, but it includes access to a variety of powerful tools that can be used for more than just storing art. The subscription includes not just OneDrive storage, but also Word, Excel, and PowerPoint desktop applications, which can be extremely useful for artists when creating documents, budgets, presentations, or planning materials.
- **File Sharing and Collaboration:** The Microsoft 365 Personal plan allows you to share files and collaborate in

real-time, making it easier to work with clients, teams, or fellow artists. This plan also provides more security features, such as advanced file versioning and higher control over access permissions.

Family Plan:

Microsoft 365 Family Plan:

The **Microsoft 365 Family Plan** is designed for families or groups who want to share storage across multiple users. With this plan, up to six people can share 1 TB of storage each, making it a great choice if you plan to share your portfolio with others or need more storage for multiple accounts.

- **Storage Space:** Each family member gets **1 TB** of storage. If you're an artist who needs to store a wide variety of media, this plan offers significant space, especially when you consider that multiple users can take advantage of the storage.
- **Cost:** While the Family Plan is more expensive than the Personal Plan, it provides the best value if multiple users in your household need access to storage. The ability to share storage is perfect for families who want to consolidate their cloud storage into a single plan.
- **File Sharing and Collaboration:** Similar to the Personal plan, this plan includes enhanced file-sharing options. It also allows users to collaborate in real-time using the Office apps, making it ideal for teams of artists or families who want to share art, documents, or other files across multiple devices.

Business Plans:

OneDrive for Business:

If you are an artist who operates a studio or has a small team working with you, the **OneDrive for Business** plan may be the best fit. This plan includes all of the features of Microsoft 365, but with additional business-focused tools.

- **Storage Space:** OneDrive for Business offers **1 TB** per user initially, and as your business grows, you can scale storage up to 5 TB per user, making it ideal for larger studios or those managing vast amounts of digital art.
- **Cost:** OneDrive for Business plans are higher in cost, but they include more advanced business collaboration features, security, and compliance tools.
- **File Sharing and Collaboration:** The OneDrive for Business plan provides advanced collaboration tools, including version control, file sharing with external users, and business-grade security. This is ideal if you're working with clients, contractors, or employees who need secure and reliable access to your artwork and documents.

Which Plan is Best for Artists?

Choosing the best OneDrive plan for your artistic needs depends on several factors, including the size of your portfolio, your storage requirements, and the level of collaboration you need. Below are some guidelines to help you make an informed decision:

For Beginners or Hobbyists:

- If you're just starting out with digital art and only have a small collection of work to store, the **Free Plan** or **100 GB Standalone Plan** could be a great starting point. These plans offer basic storage options and file-sharing capabilities, which are ideal for smaller portfolios. The 100 GB plan also provides enough room for growth if you're beginning to build a collection.

For Serious Artists or Small Studios:

- If you have a larger portfolio that includes high-resolution images, videos, or multiple projects, the **Microsoft 365 Personal Plan** with **1 TB of storage** is an excellent choice. It allows you to store a substantial amount of artwork, while also providing the added bonus of access to Microsoft Office apps. This plan is ideal for artists who want to integrate their artwork with business-related documents or presentations.

For Collaborating Artists or Art Teams:

- If you're working with other artists or sharing your portfolio with a larger team, the **Microsoft 365 Family Plan** or **OneDrive for Business Plan** would be more appropriate. These plans offer larger storage capacity and enhanced collaboration tools that make it easier to share files, track versions, and collaborate on projects in real-time.

Ultimately, selecting the right OneDrive plan comes down to understanding the size and scope of your artwork, how much collaboration you need, and what tools and features are most important for your work. By choosing the right plan, you can ensure your art portfolio is stored securely, easy to access, and ready to share with others.

Glossary of Terms

In this section, we'll define key terms and concepts used throughout the book. This glossary is designed to provide clear and concise explanations of technical terms related to OneDrive and its usage for artists. Understanding these terms will help you navigate the content of the book more easily and improve your overall experience as you build and manage your digital portfolio. Each term is explained in a straightforward manner, with a focus on practical application for artists looking to utilize OneDrive.

Cloud Storage

Cloud storage is a method of storing digital files online, rather than on physical devices like hard drives or USB drives. Files stored in the cloud can be accessed from any device with an internet connection. This allows for greater flexibility, security, and ease of sharing files with others.

Why It's Important for Artists: Cloud storage, like OneDrive, provides artists with a safe, convenient place to store large image files, design projects, and other artwork-related documents. It makes accessing your portfolio from anywhere simple, and it eliminates the risk of losing work due to device failure.

File Syncing

File syncing refers to the process of ensuring that the most recent version of a file is available on all devices where that file is stored. When you update a file on one device, syncing ensures that those changes are reflected on all devices linked to your OneDrive account.

Why It's Important for Artists: Syncing is essential for artists who work across multiple devices (such as a desktop computer, tablet, and mobile phone). It allows you to make updates to your portfolio or project files on one device, and have those changes instantly available on all other devices.

Metadata

Metadata is data that provides information about other data. In the context of digital artwork, metadata typically refers to details like the title of the artwork, the artist's name, the creation date, and relevant tags or keywords that help categorize the work.

Why It's Important for Artists: Metadata helps you stay organized by providing context for your artwork. You can quickly find and organize your files by searching for specific keywords, tags, or creation dates. This makes managing a large portfolio of artwork more efficient.

Permissions

Permissions control who can view, edit, and interact with your files. In OneDrive, you can set permissions for individual files or folders, allowing you to control whether others can just view your artwork or whether they can edit it as well.

Why It's Important for Artists: By setting the right permissions, you ensure that only the people you want to have access to your artwork can see or modify it. This is crucial when sharing sensitive or unfinished works with clients, collaborators, or exhibition curators.

Version History

Version history refers to a feature that allows you to track changes made to a file over time. In OneDrive, this means you can view and restore previous versions of a file, such as an earlier draft of your artwork.

Why It's Important for Artists: Version history provides a safeguard for your creative process. If you make a mistake or accidentally delete something important, you can quickly revert to an earlier version of your artwork. This feature is particularly useful for large projects that involve multiple revisions.

Sharing Link

A sharing link is a URL that you can generate in OneDrive to give others access to a specific file or folder. Sharing links can be set to allow others to view, edit, or comment on your artwork, depending on the permissions you set.

Why It's Important for Artists: Sharing links make it easy to distribute your work to clients, potential buyers, or collaborators without sending large email attachments. You can also control how long the link remains active and what level of access people have to your files.

Album

An album in OneDrive is a way to organize your artwork into a collection, much like a physical photo album. Albums can be customized and shared with others, making them a great tool for presenting your artwork in an organized and visually appealing manner.

Why It's Important for Artists: Creating albums allows you to group similar works together, whether by project, theme, medium, or exhibition. This helps you present a cohesive portfolio to potential clients or collectors, making it easier to showcase your work.

Folder Structure

Folder structure refers to the way in which files and folders are organized within your OneDrive account. A well-organized folder structure helps you quickly find files and keep your portfolio tidy.

Why It's Important for Artists: A clear folder structure is essential when managing a large collection of digital artwork. By using a logical hierarchy, such as categorizing your artwork by medium, year, or project, you can easily access specific files whenever you need them.

File Sharing

File sharing is the process of distributing files to others via OneDrive. You can share files directly with specific people, generate sharing links for public access, or even embed files in websites or social media.

Why It's Important for Artists: File sharing allows you to collaborate with other artists, show your portfolio to potential buyers, or send artwork to clients. It's a flexible way to make your work accessible to others while controlling who can view or modify the files.

Collaboration

Collaboration in OneDrive refers to working together on files in real-time. Multiple people can edit a shared document or artwork simultaneously, and each change is automatically synced across all users' devices.

Why It's Important for Artists: Collaboration is key when working on joint projects or commissions. With OneDrive, you can easily work with other artists, designers, or clients, making edits and exchanging feedback in real time without worrying about version control.

Backup

A backup is a duplicate copy of your files stored in a secure location to protect against data loss. OneDrive automatically backs up your files to the cloud, but you can also manually create backups to external drives or other cloud services.

Why It's Important for Artists: Regular backups ensure that your artwork is safe from unexpected data loss, such as hardware failure or accidental deletion. By backing up your files to OneDrive and other secure locations, you safeguard your creative work.

Syncing Across Devices

Syncing across devices means ensuring that the files you store in OneDrive are available on all devices you use. Once a file is uploaded to OneDrive, it's accessible on any device you link to your account, such as a smartphone, tablet, or laptop.

Why It's Important for Artists: This feature allows artists to work seamlessly across different devices, ensuring that they can access and edit their files no matter where they are. For example, you can start working on your portfolio at home and finish it while traveling.

Public vs. Private Sharing

Public sharing refers to making your files or albums accessible to anyone with the link, while private sharing restricts access to specific people you invite.

Why It's Important for Artists: Public sharing can be used to showcase your work to a wide audience, while private sharing is more appropriate for confidential or unfinished work that you don't want to be widely accessible. Managing these settings gives you control over who can view or interact with your artwork.

Cloud-Enabled Devices

Cloud-enabled devices are devices that are capable of syncing files with cloud storage platforms like OneDrive. These devices include smartphones, tablets, laptops, and desktops.

Why It's Important for Artists: Using cloud-enabled devices makes it easier to work on your artwork wherever you are. You can access and update your portfolio from any device, ensuring you can continue working on your art regardless of location.

www.ingramcontent.com/pod-product-compliance
Lightning Source LLC
LaVergne TN
LVHW022342060326
832902LV00022B/4197